Praise for
DEVELOPING EXEMPLARY PERFORMANCE ONE PERSON AT A TIME and MICHAEL SABBAG

"This book should be required reading for anyone who manages people. Until now, managing performance was mostly a rearward-facing exercise that often put managers at odds with their workers. Sabbag gives managers a new roadmap to proactively improve performance by creating a partnership between themselves and their workers that builds upon strengths and provides development opportunities. *Developing Exemplary Performance One Person at a Time* will be used for decades to come by organizations that wish to become more successful and competitive."

—Jim Riley, Founder and CEO, Learn.com, Inc.

"In my HR role, I am constantly struggling to explain to leaders that training is not the only answer for performance issues, and may often not be the right answer. This book lays out a model to help leaders diagnose the real reasons why people may not be performing to standards and allows proper action planning for improvement."

—Alicia Goodman, Senior Vice President, Human Resources, TNS

"Going far beyond existing models of performance development, Sabbag provides leaders with both a process roadmap and a practical toolbox for strength-based employee development. His user-friendly Seven Step Exemplary Performance Model serves as a performance development toolbox for leaders. Using Sabbag's Model, the leader can more accurately diagnose the root cause performance factors and then select performance development tools that are highly targeted and relevant to the individual."

—Rita Smith, Vice President of Enterprise Learning, Ingersoll Rand Company

"Michael Sabbag is a seasoned, authentic leader with an amazing grasp of the performance challenges facing businesses today and an even more amazing ability to clearly articulate how to diagnose and solve those challenges to yield exemplary results. *Developing Exemplary Performance One Person at a Time* is intelligent, practical and easy to understand."

—Sharon Wingron, CPLP, Leadership Consultant and President of Wings of Success, LLC

Developing Exemplary Performance
One Person at a Time

Developing
Exemplary
Performance
One Person
at a Time

Michael Sabbag

an imprint of Nicholas Brealey Publishing
Boston • London

First published by Davies-Black, an imprint of Nicholas Brealey Publishing, in 2009.

20 Park Plaza, Suite 1115A	3–5 Spafield Street, Clerkenwell
Boston, MA 02116, USA	London, EC1R 4QB, UK
Tel: + 617-523-3801	Tel: +44-(0)-207-239-0360
Fax: + 617-523-3708	Fax: +44-(0)-207-239-0370

www.nicholasbrealey.com

Special discounts on bulk quantities of Davies-Black books are available to corporations, professional associations, and other organizations. For details, contact us at 888-273-2539.

Printed in the United States of America

13 12 11 10 09   10 9 8 7 6 5 4 3 2 1

ISBN: 978-0-89106-249-3

Library of Congress Cataloging-in-Publication Data
Sabbag, Michael
Developing exemplary performance one person at a time / Michael Sabbag.
    p. cm.
Includes bibliographical references and index.
ISBN 978-0-89106-249-3 (hardcover)
1. Performance—Management. 2. Employee motivation. 3. Supervision of employees.
I. Title.
HF5549.5.P35S23 2008
658.3'14—dc22   2008038675

FIRST EDITION
First printing 2009

Contents

List of Tables and Figures   ix
Acknowledgments   xi
About the Author   xiii
Introduction   xv

Part One: A New Way to Achieve Exemplary Performance
1. Principles of the Exemplary Performance Model   3
2. The Exemplary Performance Model Explained   23

Part Two: The Exemplary Performance Factors
3. The Talent and Fit Factor   43
4. The Environment Factor   65
5. The Tools and Resources Factor   87
6. The Systems and Processes Factor   103
7. The Clear Expectations and Accountability Factor   121
8. The Knowledge and Skills Factor   141
9. The Motivation Factor   155

Part Three: Applying the Model
10. The Development Process Step by Step   175
11. Rolling Out the Model in the Real World   197

Appendix A: Exemplary Performance Model
    Increases Sales at City Furniture   211
Appendix B: Questions for Use in Diagnosing
    Performance Factors   219
Notes   223
Index   229

List of Tables and Figures

Tables

1. The Seven Performance Factors Defined   33
2. Prerequisites for Using the Exemplary Performance Model   38
3. What Makes Up Talent?   46
4. Examples of Organizational Culture   67
5. Components of the Personal Environment   72
6. Tools for Addressing the Environment Factor   80
7. Examples of Tools and Resources Issues   92
8. Examples of Creative Workarounds   98
9. Formal Versus Informal Processes   106
10. Process Improvement in Action   112
11. Tools for Leveraging Exemplary Performance   117
12. Examples of Clear Expectations   123
13. Examples of Accountability   128
14. Knowledge and Skills Tools for Addressing Exemplary Strengths   153
15. Examples of Intangible Rewards   167
16. Questions Asked at Each Step of the Model   192
17. Examples of Tasks Aligned with Organizational Goal   201
18. Challenges and Solutions for Working with the Model   205
19. Difference Between Study and Control Locations in Average Sales per Employee per Month   215

Figures

1. Key Principles of the Exemplary Performance Model   12
2. Target Employees for Exemplary Performance Model   19
3. Exemplary Performance Development Cycle   26
4. The Seven Performance Factors   32
5. Tools of the Exemplary Performance Model   35
6. Interpersonal Relationships That Contribute
to the Work Environment   69
7. The Exemplary Performance Model Process   182

Acknowledgments

This book was made possible only by the contribution of many special people in my life, whom I would like to acknowledge.

- My wife, Elizabeth, supported me through the long hours I put in writing this book in addition to my full-time job. Without her love, encouragement, and support, this would not have been possible.

- My family always made me feel that it was a foregone conclusion that the book would get published, even before I had a publisher.

- Suzanne Murray and Neville Uhles, of StyleMatters Writing Services, exhibited professionalism, intelligence, and exemplary talents in writing and editing. They helped shape this book and teamed up with me to make it something we are proud of.

- Laura Lawson, of Davies-Black Publishing, went above and beyond helping to educate me on the ins and outs of publishing. Her guidance was excellent and incredibly helpful.

- Learn.com has completely supported my endeavor with its encouragement, time, and funding. It is an exemplary organization, and I am proud to work with its true professionals.

About the Author

Michael Sabbag has more than twenty years of experience in the fields of talent management, organizational development, and training. He is an established speaker at the national and local levels on topics such as performance development, strategic planning, and measuring ROI for training. He is active in ASTD and is a member of the ASTD National Advisor for Chapters team.

As Vice President of Talent Management at Learn.com, Sabbag is responsible for the consulting team and all internal HR and talent management activities. Prior to joining Learn.com, he was president of Performance & Training Consultants, Inc., a consulting firm focused on helping clients reach exemplary performance levels through their people. His clients included organizations large (Centex Homes, AdvancedAuto, and SimplexGrinnell) and small (BankAtlantic and Children's Services Council of Palm Beach).

Previously, Sabbag held the positions of Sales Trainer, Regional Leadership Instructor, and Manager of Leadership Development at Comcast. He also led a companywide team that created the infrastructure for training throughout the 40,000-employee organization. His extensive training experience includes work as a reservations trainer in the travel industry and as a training manager in the auto rental industry.

Sabbag holds a Bachelor of Science degree from Florida State University and a Master of Arts degree from University of the Pacific. He is certified as a Senior Professional in Human Resources by the Society for Human Resource Management.

Introduction

As a professional in human resources (HR), learning, and organization development for the past twenty years, I have found that the impact leaders have on the performance of their employees is the most critical issue in business. This impact matters more than strategy, the business environment, or any other issue that may challenge an organization. Through the effective development and management of employees, an organization can surmount any obstacle and achieve success. The question is, which approach or model is the best one for developing employee performance at your organization?

There are several models out there for you to choose from: the human performance technology model,[1] Pipe and Manger's model,[2] and Gilbert's behavior-engineering model,[3] as well as the strength-based approach provided by authors such as Marcus Buckingham.[4] I am excited to add a new model, the Exemplary Performance Model, which builds on the best parts of previous perform-

> *The impact leaders have on the performance of their employees is the most critical issue in business.*

ance development thinking and closes the gaps left by others. The model has emerged from my own research and experience and has come about to fill a practical need for a relatively simple, straightforward, and effective means of developing employees.

The Trouble with Training

Long before I began using the Exemplary Performance Model, one area of my work involved teaching leadership classes and training people on leadership skills. The people who attended my classes seemed to enjoy the sessions, rated the training highly, and would return to learn about other topics. Over time, the numbers of attendees grew and grew.

Yet when following up, I discovered that attendees' on-the-job performance was improving only slightly after the training. This frustrated me. True, the slight improvements in performance often yielded a significant return on investment. (In some cases, each dollar spent on a class yielded over a thousand dollars in savings to the organization.) But I knew the potential existed to improve participants' performance much more substantially.

This frustration was certainly present in the situation in one of my former jobs as a regional manager of leadership development, where I trained some two hundred VPs, managers, and supervisors. Often, these leaders walked away from the training excited to apply what they had learned. And yet, time and again, they went back their departments and operated exactly as they had before the training. As a result, their performance did not improve much. Although the training received high marks from attendees, the classes didn't seem to be yielding a significant increase in performance. And those leaders would come back to me and complain that their employees needed my training—rather than realizing that they still needed to make changes in their own behavior. I kept thinking that if these leaders could not change their behaviors after training, why should we expect that their employees would alter their behaviors after the same classes?

> *Performance can be addressed with the right tools only if a leader first knows what performance factor serves as the root cause of performance.*

Capitalizing on Strengths

From my recurrent frustration I realized two things:

1. There was no organizational support for leaders to engage in the new behaviors they had learned—no reinforcement or accountability for whether they actually used their newly acquired skills.

2. Training was often sought as the solution for improving performance when, in fact, training wasn't the remedy that was truly needed. If employees lacked skills or knowledge of how to perform their jobs, training was very useful. But there were many other reasons why employees might not be performing up to expectations: ineffective company processes, lack of re-

sources, family problems, or any of a whole host of other issues. If any of these other factors was the issue, training—no matter how good or how much—would never solve the problem.

I couldn't blame leaders for trying to solve employee performance problems with the universal cry of "send 'em to training." This was the way things had always been done in many organizations, where people learned their leadership skills by modeling after the leaders above them. And although performance models have increasingly acknowledged that there's more to improving performance than training, these models have often stopped short of specifically explaining how to identify and address non-training-related issues.

A New Model for Performance

It was from my original discovery that training was often not the antidote to performance problems (a discovery that coincided with what was happening in the fields of HR, learning, and organization development), that I eventually created the Exemplary Performance Model. The aims of this new model are:

- **To diagnose the root cause** of performance (the performance factor), exploring many more potential causes than just skills and knowledge
- **To develop or leverage performance** by addressing the diagnosed performance factor through the use of targeted tools

As those of you familiar with the performance development literature will discover, this model is not revolutionary but rather evolutionary. For example, the model capitalizes on the notion that numerous factors for performance exist, as highlighted in the human performance technology model.[5] In addition, the model aligns with the strengths-based movement[6] by focusing on strengths rather than weaknesses during the performance development process.

Recognizing Many Possible Causes for Performance

Leaders, by sending employees to training, have traditionally assumed that employees perform poorly because they do not have enough skills and knowledge to perform at a higher level. But there are many possible reasons why performance occurs at a given level. The Exemplary Performance Model presents the seven different factors that affect performance:

- Talent and fit
- Environment
- Tools and resources
- Systems and processes
- Clear expectations and accountability
- Knowledge and skills
- Motivation

The value of recognizing the multitude of possible performance factors goes far beyond mere understanding. The value lies in the results of this understanding: specifically, guidance for creating a targeted action plan to achieve exemplary performance. Performance can be addressed with the right tools only if a leader first knows what performance factor serves as the root cause of performance. If someone lacks motivation, for example, sending him to training will likely do very little to increase motivation. Instead, other solutions will be more effective—such as offering the employee regular praise or involvement in contests that get him excited about performing.

Capitalizing on Strengths

Although the model can be used to address employee weaknesses, the main focus of the model is on strengths. This is because only strengths have the potential to be developed to the exemplary level. Research has shown that individuals' strengths and weaknesses can be traced in part to the brain;[7] the exemplary performance model acknowledges the biological basis for strengths and weaknesses by encouraging leaders to focus on developing strengths to the exemplary level and accepting that weaknesses may never improve beyond a level of sufficiency.

Thus, by focusing on strengths rather than on weaknesses for performance development, you will tend to get more return on your investment in the development process. In addition, employees are likely to remain more motivated and engaged in a strengths-based process because they will feel valued when their strengths are noticed, appreciated, and capitalized on. Finally, understanding why an employee performs so well in a given area may enable you to foster this kind of excellence in other employees.

High Performance Meets Strategic Goals

Without adequate employee performance, strategy doesn't get executed, and when strategy doesn't get executed, organizations can't meet goals or succeed. As Larry Bossidy and Ram Charan note, "Execution is the greatest unaddressed issue in the business world today. Its absence is the single biggest obstacle to success."[8] Interestingly, Ernst & Young reported, in a study of 275 portfolio managers, that "the ability to execute strategy was more important than the quality of the strategy itself."[9] In other words, the way that people put strategy into action through their performance can be more significant than the content of the strategy.

The following example illustrates this point:

Imagine that you own a local pizza parlor and that your strategy is to make your restaurant as fun and comfortable for families with small children as possible. You fill the restaurant with colorful decorations, you provide a big basket of toys for children to play with, and you install a television that you set to a cartoon channel. You train your waiters to be friendly to children and to offer each one a balloon when they take a table's orders.

Yet you discover over time that many of your employees forget to offer a balloon, and some of your employees change the TV from the cartoon channel to other programming. In addition, the cleaning crew never remembers to wipe the toys down at the end of the day, and the toys have begun to look dirty and old. In short, your employees are not performing up to your standards, your strategy isn't executed as you had envisioned it, and your resulting revenues reflect this lack of strategic execution.

The pizza parlor example is a simple one, but it underscores how successful strategic execution hinges on high performance by employees.

Although I do not often speak specifically of strategy in this book, my purpose is to improve strategic execution—by helping people perform at the exemplary level in the workplace. When employees achieve their professional goals at work, departmental goals are met. When departments achieve their goals, the company in turn executes and achieves its strategy. When employee goals are set at the exemplary level, organizations themselves become exemplary. The results of performance, good or bad, will ripple throughout the whole organization.

About This Book

The Exemplary Performance Model is designed to assist those in a leadership role with developing the performance of their employees. The model's use is not restricted to the business setting. While my hope is that this book will provide thousands of leaders at all levels of organizations with valuable guidance, the first audience for this book is one particular set of practitioners—professionals in human resources, organization development, and learning and development.

Those of you in this group are often tasked with the responsibility of helping leaders improve employees' performance, and you are the ones who often have to deal with the undiscerning "send 'em to training" mentality. Although you likely appreciate the value of training and perhaps even spend a good portion of your time developing and leading training yourselves, your ultimate goal is to develop employee performance in the best way possible. The model will help you work with your organization's leaders to find the best solutions for developing employee performance—whether training or something else. Using the model, you will be able to guide leaders to consider all of the possible causes for employee performance and then work with these leaders to apply targeted, relevant solutions that can bring about significant performance development. In addition, you will be viewed as a business partner rather than as a "necessary cost."

If you are a leader who is directly responsible for the performance of others, this book can be equally helpful. Your role is to execute strategy through the people on your team. Since this happens only when your people perform well, your role in developing employee performance is critical to the success of the organization. The tools and process presented here will help you develop people to achieve performance at the exemplary level.

You will notice that certain terms are used that require definition. Leader is not meant to communicate that an individual has leadership qualities but indicates that the person is someone who leads another person or group of people. Tool is used to label a method, technique, or process that is used to yield a result. For example, a leader often uses coaching to develop a skill or set of skills in an individual. Coaching is a tool used for development. The tools covered here—and there are many—are designed to help leaders address performance issues with just the right remedy. Instead of simply throwing training at an employee, leaders who use this model will have a variety of options for how to assist employees in developing their performance—not for variety's sake but to ensure effectiveness of solution.

I have organized this book along the following lines: in chapter 1, I present a discussion of the seven principles of the Exemplary Performance Model. In chapter 2, I provide an overview of how to use the model by describing the steps involved in diagnosing and developing employee performance. In chapters 3 through 9, I review each of the seven performance factors that potentially lie at the heart of a given performance problem. In chapters 10 and 11, I go into further depth in the use of the model and discuss alternate applications. Finally, in appendix A, I provide hands-on advice for using the model in the workplace by presenting a case study detailing its use at an organization. In appendix B, I summarize the diagnostic questions to determine the key factors in performance.

In the book in its entirety I provide the guidance needed to roll out the Exemplary Performance Model in the workplace and to educate organizational leaders on its use and benefits. I also provide leaders themselves with the information they need to begin using the model to effectively develop their employees' performance to the exemplary level.

Conclusion

The people who have attended my training classes over the years have typically come to each class looking for an answer. Some have wanted to get better at hiring people. Others have hoped to learn an effective way to coach employees for development. And still others have sought ways to deal with employees who didn't seem to care about their performance and therefore weren't performing well. As someone who's passionate about performance, I'm thrilled to offer you a powerful new approach for developing your employees and achieving exemplary performance one employee at a time. I've seen the value of the Exemplary Performance Model in action, and I continue to marvel at its power to help employees and companies reach peak performance. It is my hope that, after reading this book and applying the model in your workplace, you will have a similar experience.

Part I

A New Way to Achieve Exemplary Performance

1

Principles of the Exemplary Performance Model

As a leader, the single most important thing you can do for your organization is drive the execution of strategy. No matter what you do and no matter what your level in the organization, this is your most critical role: to drive execution in yourself, in your peers, in your leaders, and in your direct reports.

Strategic execution results from performing well, and performing well comes from a variety of factors—such as having the right talent and fit for a job, having adequate tools and resources, having useful systems and processes, and having sufficient knowledge and skills. The model I present in this book is built around these and other factors of performance so that you can address performance at its root and develop appropriate action plans that help you foster exemplary performance in each of your employees. As your employees move toward the exemplary level of performance, so will your department's ability to execute strategy at the exemplary level. It all begins with understanding which cause is at the heart of performance. From there, the rest will follow.

When Employees Are Seen as the Problem

It is easy to confuse the causes of performance that can impede achieving an exemplary level of strategic execution.

When I was teenager, I worked at a local drugstore called Gray Drugs. One day, I was in charge of running the register out front. Things were going well until the end of my shift, when I counted the money in the register and realized that the total was twenty dollars and two cents lower than what it was supposed to be. In response, my manager began writing up a report on me, per store policy.

I knew I hadn't pocketed the money, but I did worry that I might have given someone the wrong change. Even though I'd never been more than fifty cents off at the end of my shift, the numbers didn't lie. Just as I was ready to give up on solving the mystery of what had happened, I pulled the inner drawer out of the register and discovered that a twenty dollar bill had somehow gotten pushed underneath.

Of course, my manager threw the report in the trash. But the incident left a bad taste in my mouth. My manager had counted the money in the drawer only once and then immediately gone to writing up the incident report, without taking any time to figure out what might have happened. He seemed perfectly happy to assume that I was in the wrong. The demoralizing effect of this incident led me not to put in the extra effort that I had before the cash-register incident. In short, my performance diminished.

Why did my performance at Gray's initially seem to "fail"? In large part, it failed because the process of signing off the register did not involve lifting the drawer to check underneath for missing bills as it probably should have. If store processes had included this step, I would not have been twenty dollars under on my drawer, and future employee performance regarding accuracy at the cash register would have been improved. Yet my manager never considered changing store processes. He just blamed me for being bad at signing off the register.

This approach of blaming the employee still occurs in the modern workplace. Quite often, employees are seen as problems rather than as resources. Sometimes this occurs because it's the easiest solution and one that lets a leader abdicate responsibility and avoid having to actively engage in addressing a performance issue. Other times, this occurs because leaders are simply copying the same limited leadership techniques they learned from their own managers. If these leaders had more techniques, they'd use them; because they don't, they miss factors external to the employee that might be the key source of performance issues—factors that the leaders themselves could help address and improve.

> *As a leader, the single most important thing you can do for your organization is drive the execution of strategy.*

Key Concepts from the Model

There are certain key concepts that will serve as a foundation to your understanding to the model. These are presented below.

PERFORMANCE DEFINED

In lay terms, performance is the degree to which someone "gets things done." In the language of the profession, performance refers to how a person is executing key responsibilities and tasks relative to the standards set for those responsibilities and tasks.

Performance is a neutral term. It is not until a descriptor is added to the term *performance* that we get a sense of its value. If an employee yields the results we expect for him or her, or returns outcomes above those expectations, we call this "good performance." If an employee yields results that are below our expectations, we call the person's performance "poor," "bad," or "lacking." Performance can be better understood by breaking down the particulars of how performance gets measured.

Metrics

To assess performance, we first need *metrics*, that is, categories of measurement. For example, to measure my performance on the client progress reports I turn in each week at my job, my manager uses the metrics of timeliness, quality, and content. Specifically, my manager assesses:

- Whether my report is turned in on time (metric 1)
- Whether its quality is good (metric 2)
- Whether its content is satisfactory (metric 3)

If my manager were examining my performance in terms of how well I bring in new client business, he would use different metrics, such as the number of new clients I bring to the firm each month.

Standards

In addition to metrics, we need *standards*. Standards describe the level at which each metric needs to be met for performance to be considered adequate. For example, in order for my performance on progress reports to be satisfactory, my weekly reports have to meet the following standards for timeliness, quality, and content:

- They need to be turned in by Friday (standard for metric 1, timeliness).
- The data needs to be accurate (standard for metric 2, quality).
- They need to cover other content areas such as the number of client interactions, number of completed sales, and my observations about our products (standard for metric 3, content).

If my performance as measured by these metrics meets or exceeds these standards, my manager considers my performance for writing up progress reports to be satisfactory; if my performance in this area falls below these standards, my manager sees my performance as needing improvement.

Without standards, metrics are meaningless. For example, U.S. state troopers measure drivers' speeds in miles per hour (a metric), but without a standard (a speed limit), officers would be unable to judge whether a driver is obeying the law (or "performing" properly). Just imagine sending a traffic officer out to a city street or highway with a radar gun and asking him to write tickets to speeders without informing the officer of the speed limit in that zone. Should the officer ticket those driving 35 miles an hour? 45 miles an hour? 50 miles an hour? The speeds of drivers would be meaningless to the officer without a standard (speed limit) to judge their performance/ behavior (speed) against. It's the same for managers who want to assess their employees' performance. Managers need to know not only what metrics should be used to measure employee performance but also what standards are considered acceptable for that performance. Such metrics and standards are necessary to assess an employee's current performance and thus are prerequisites for using the present model.

LEVELS OF PERFORMANCE

As we begin to see, performance can be labeled by degree (e.g., good versus bad). In developing the Exemplary Performance Model, I have identified four levels of performance:

- Lagging
- At-standards
- Exemplary
- Cutting-edge

Lagging Performance

When someone is not consistently executing his key responsibilities at the standards set by a company, that person's performance is lagging. Let's look at a restaurant example. If all the waiters at a given restaurant chain are tasked with selling at least two of each menu entrée every night (to reduce food waste) and if the employee you are working with to develop performance sells only one of each entrée every night, his performance is considered lagging (not meeting organizational standards). Lagging performance can occur for any number of reasons: work environment, process, skills and knowledge, or something else. We'll discuss the seven possible causes (factors) for performance in the next chapter.

At-Standards Performance

At-standards performance occurs when an employee consistently executes his or her key responsibilities in a way that either meets organizational standards or falls slightly above standards. Managers and leaders are typically quite happy when their employees are performing at standards because it means that organizational goals are being met through the employees' work. One area of performance that is important at my particular job is workshop presentation skills, and one of the metrics used to measure my performance in that area is the ratings I receive from workshop participants on the evaluation form. My performance is considered to be at standards if I receive an average score of 4 on a scale of 1 to 5.

Exemplary Performance

Although at-standards performance is a great place to start, in order to be highly successful, organizations need to learn how to develop their employees to the next level of performance: exemplary performance. With the right tools and guidance, it is completely feasible for organizations to develop exemplary performance in the majority of their employees.

Exemplary performance occurs when an employee consistently executes a key responsibility or task at a level that matches the level of individuals who are considered to be the best in the industry (exemplars). Note that the exemplary level is almost always *significantly above the typical standards set by most organizations,*[1] which tend to define standards on the basis of the average outcomes of all employees. In fact, in my discussions with hundreds of learning and performance professionals, I have yet to see an organization that sets its standards of performance at the exemplary level.

Exemplary performance occurs when an employee consistently executes at a level that matches the level of those who are the best in the industry.

Now, let's look at an example of exemplary performance. If I regularly score an average of 4.9 on my evaluation reports for workshop presentations, my performance is exemplary because only the best presenters consistently score an overall average of 4.9. Note that bursts of performance significantly above the standard (one presentation with an average evaluation score of 5, compared to most of my performances, if I had an average evaluation score of 3.5, for example) do not make my performance exemplary; only if my performance is *consistently* at the highest level can it be considered exemplary.

So, in determining whether someone is performing at an exemplary level, we compare her performance to those individuals in the industry who are seen as being best-in-class for that particular task or key responsibility. Note that by using the superlative *best,* I do not mean to say that only one person in a department can have exemplary performance, but that exemplary performers are the cream of the crop: there can certainly be more than one exemplary performer, but *all* of these individuals perform significantly above normal standards.

To better understand this idea of best-in-class and cream of the crop, think about professional golfers. Tiger Woods would doubtless be considered an exemplary performer because he consistently performs significantly under par (which is great, in golf). But Tiger Woods is not the only professional golfer who tends to consistently perform under par. There are other golfers who meet this description—such as Vijay Singh and Phil Mickelson—so they are exemplary performers too. As Stanley Eitzen noted, the top one hundred professional golfers play, on average, "within two strokes of each other for every eighteen holes."[2] Though Woods wins a lot of the competitions, many of the other professional golfers on the circuit are exemplary performers as well.

The moral here for the corporate world is that it's possible to have many exemplary performers on your team, not just one star player. Why "settle" for just Tiger Woods, when you can have Vijay Singh and Phil Mickelson as well? With the right tools and guidance, you can develop many, if not all, of your employees to the exemplary performance level.

Nonetheless, exemplary performance is not common at most organizations. This is not because exemplary performance is infeasible or unattainable but because leaders lack knowledge, tools, and guidance on how to develop exemplary performance in their employees. If you look at highly successful organizations, you will discover that the leaders in those organizations have figured out how to develop exemplary performance in the majority of employees. These exemplary performers drive these organizations forward. For example, Disney invests a lot in its people, is well known for being a great place to work, and has a large number of exemplary performers.[3] Disney's stock also increased in value by 91 percent from 2003 to 2008 as the company's organizational performance improved.[4]

The standard of exemplary performance has yet to be embraced throughout the majority of organizations, however. Instead, most organizations set standards on the basis of the average outcomes of all employees, a benchmark that often falls well beneath the exemplary level. As research has shown, people perform up to expectations, so leaders should leverage this reality by expecting excellence during the development process.[5] Ask, and ye shall receive.

Cutting-Edge Performance

When performance exceeds even the exemplary level, I call this type of performance cutting edge. Cutting-edge performance is truly rare, but it exists nonetheless. Cutting-edge performance occurs when someone executes his or her key responsibilities in a way that changes one's view of what people are capable of. Outcomes of cutting-edge performance not only significantly exceed standards (as exemplary performance does), but they raise the standards for what can be expected of people in the future by changing people's understanding of what can actually be accomplished. In that sense, cutting-edge performance can also be called evolutionary.

A great example of cutting-edge performance occurred when the four-minute mile was broken in the mid-twentieth century. During the first century that times were recorded for the mile for professional runners, times were stuck above four minutes.[6] The four-minute mile was said by some to be unbreakable. But in 1954 Roger Bannister of the United Kingdom ran the mile in 3:59.4 minutes. Bannister's performance was cutting edge. The top runners—those who were already exemplary—would now try to beat a new time standard for the mile, less than four minutes, that was previously thought impossible. This is just one example of how cutting-edge performance both helps standards for performance to evolve and creates new paradigms of performance.

There are techniques for developing cutting-edge performance, but they will not be my focus in this book. Since most organizations hold their employees only to *meeting* performance standards rather than to significantly *exceeding* them, I will focus instead on helping you move your employees from at-standards performance to exemplary performance. (Interestingly, cutting-edge performance may occur as a result of attempts to achieve exemplary performance because, when people are striving to match the best of the best, they occasionally end up exceeding the exemplary standard.)

Returns on Investment
in Exemplary Performance

Significant returns can be achieved when leaders invest their time, energy, and resources in using the Exemplary Performance Model to develop employees from at-standards to exemplary performance. For example, one particular supervisor in a call center used this model to help his employees more effectively troubleshoot customer issues, which in turn decreased the number of service technician visits to customer homes. This particular performance improvement, which involved only twelve employees, saved the company $10,080 in the first year. If the improvement had also been applied to the other eighty-four employees in the call center, savings would have been $80,640.

Just imagine having a bunch of Tiger Woodses running around your organization. The degree of departmental or organizational success you'd experience would be enormous. As you reflect on your own organization, perhaps you're starting to see the possibilities for success that the present model can offer your leaders and employees. I've seen those possibilities fulfilled after using the model myself many times, and I've seen them fulfilled for others after they learned how to use it; I am confident that you will soon see similar success.

Foundational Principles of the
Exemplary Performance Model

The Exemplary Performance Model is built on seven key principles, which are shown in figure 1 on the following page.

The seven principles in figure 1 reflect the defining aspects of the model and highlight the philosophy behind its process and steps. Let's talk about each of these principles now, in more depth.

1. MANY POSSIBLE ROOT CAUSES FOR PERFORMANCE EXIST

Although performance development approaches of the past have mostly assumed performance can be traced back to one factor—skills and knowledge—the reality is that the sources for the character of performance are many and depend on a given person, that person's situ-

FIGURE 1 **Key Principles of the Exemplary Performance Model**

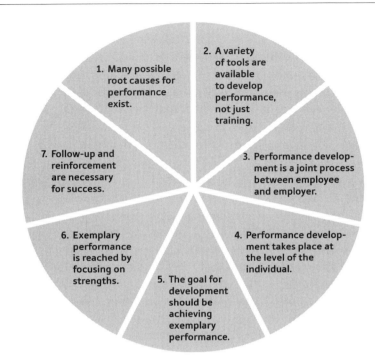

ation, and the performance task or skill being measured. In other words, if you were to target the same exact performance issue for three different people, you would likely find different primary causes (factors) for each person's performance.

For example, let's say that you are the director of the advertising department at a newspaper and you decide to target the same area of potential improvement in performance for three of your advertising sales reps: bringing in new client business, as measured by sales volume. When you work through the performance development process, it's very possible that each person will evidence a different root cause (key factor) behind his or her performance. Perhaps one employee is deathly afraid of making calls to cold leads, in which case *talent and fit* would be the performance factor at issue. That is, the employee is not well suited to a sales job (lack of fit), and this affects her performance.

Perhaps the second employee does not have an accurate price list, in which case she does not have the necessary *tools and resources* to do her job. Finally, the third employee may not realize that he should be using the company's standard script to sell business to new clients, in which case the *clear expectations* factor is at issue. He doesn't understand that using the script is a required part of his job that will help him perform better. As you can see, the primary cause of performance problems can vary greatly according to the individual. Knowing what performance area you want to target (increasing sales to new clients, in this case) is not sufficient for developing performance; you need to learn more about which factor is primarily driving or constraining that performance so that you can accurately address that factor.

2. DEVELOPMENT IS NOT JUST ABOUT TRAINING

Once you determine the cause of performance (the key performance factor), you will be ready to create an action plan to address that factor. But what kind of action plan should you create? Which set of steps in an action plan will yield the desired increase in performance? As I stated earlier, when leaders see problems in performance, they often jump right to the training solution. Sending employees to training implies that the key performance factor at issue is a lack of skills and knowledge. Leaders figure that if they give their employees more skills and knowledge, performance will automatically improve. Once you consciously recognize that performance problems can occur for other reasons, however, it becomes clearer that training will not always offer the most effective solution to performance problems.

Let's return to the example of the advertising sales reps. It is probably not surprising to you that each performance factor evidenced by these reps will require a different set of tools to address it. For example, to address talent and fit, you might need to rework a person's job profile to eliminate areas that the person isn't good at; to address tools and resources, you might need to provide the employee with an updated price list; and to address clear expectations and accountability, you might need to show the employee the key responsibilities in his job profile. Each situation—with its key performance factor—requires a separate set of tools to develop performance.

Although there are many, the tools offered by the Exemplary Performance Model are just a starting point. Because they link back to specific performance factors that help focus brainstorming, these tools can inspire your thinking about other tools that will be useful in developing performance. Once you know which performance factor is at play, you will be free to brainstorm with the employee about tools that can be applied to address that performance factor, rather than using only those tools listed in the model. You will learn about the set of tools that is best suited to address a given factor in chapters 3 through 9, which cover each factor in depth.

3. PERFORMANCE DEVELOPMENT IS A JOINT PROCESS

It's often easiest to blame the employee for lagging performance, as shown by the story of my work at the drugstore. Yet the literature has revealed that many performance factors extend beyond the employee's locus of control such that the employee *and* the leader are jointly responsible for addressing the factor.[7] Sometimes, for example, employees don't have the information they need to perform well. Although the employee is responsible for requesting this information, you are equally responsible for supplying it or for helping the employee gain access to it. Once you realize the degree to which you play a role in your employees' development, you will be in a better position to create effective action plans because you will understand what your own role is in developing performance. In sum, performance development can occur only if a *partnership* is created between you and your employee. So it is not just employees who may need to start doing things differently to improve performance; often, you, too, will need to get involved to provide employees with the solutions and support needed to raise performance to the next level.

4. PERFORMANCE DEVELOPMENT TAKES PLACE AT THE LEVEL OF THE INDIVIDUAL

In the past, many leaders have applied a collective rather than an individualized approach to performance improvement. The mentality has been not only to send a specific employee to training if he needs to improve performance, but to send *all* employees to training. In others words, instead of detecting that each employee's performance occurs on the basis of unique factors, many leaders assume that the root cause for employee performance is common to everyone in the group or department. Statements like the following are made:

- "Everyone needs to get refreshed through a training course."
- "No one here is motivated to do a good job."
- "We just don't have any talented people."

Sweeping generalizations are often made regarding employee performance—to the detriment of the performance development process. Yet this generalizing is like a doctor writing the same prescription for all of her patients before examining each of them individually.

Inherent in the Exemplary Performance Model is the notion that performance development is best addressed at the level of the individual rather than that of the group. Given that there are many possible reasons why performance occurs as it does, a one-size-fits-the- whole-department approach cannot possibly cater to each individual's unique reason for performance. In addition, employees' strengths and weaknesses are vastly different. While one employee may need to develop customer service skills, another may need to focus on better time management. Clearly, each of these employees will benefit from a different kind of action plan for development.

5. THE GOAL FOR DEVELOPMENT SHOULD BE ACHIEVING EXEMPLARY PERFORMANCE

As I mentioned earlier, most organizations set their performance standards at a level that is far below exemplary. This is not inherently a bad thing, as long as the organizational standards created do indeed map to the outcomes required by the organization for baseline success and as long as these standards are not intended to define the ultimate goal of performance development. It is fine to judge people against such organizational standards during the performance *management* process. The problem arises when organizations feel it is sufficient during the performance *development* process to guide employees only up to the level of organizational standards rather than to encourage employees to achieve exemplary performance.

Perhaps it is easy for leaders to fall into this "below-exemplary" snare because they often have the mistaken notion that exemplars in an organization must be rare—only one Tiger Woods—and so they don't encourage the remainder of employees to achieve exemplary performance. Yet, in reality, most employees do have the potential to achieve exemplary performance—not for every single task that makes up their jobs, but for those that match their strengths. A first step in achieving exemplary performance is to set goals designed to yield outcomes that match those of exemplars in the industry.

6. EXEMPLARY PERFORMANCE IS REACHED BY FOCUSING ON STRENGTHS

The natural assumption about performance development is that one will be focusing solely on those areas where employees are weak or lagging. As the strengths-based movement has revealed, however, there is real value to leveraging employees' strengths.[8] Not only will employees stay engaged in the performance development process because they feel valued, but they will gain useful insight into how they can capitalize on strengths to execute strategy, and you will gain a greater return on your investment. It's therefore important not to ignore individuals' strengths or to take them for granted. Instead, you will benefit from assessing the strengths of employees in partnership with them and then determining whether they can build on these strengths to further develop performance and to better execute strategy. While growth areas (what I later define as "expandable strengths") will get targeted by the Exemplary Performance Model, note that the present model does not encourage leaders and employees to target growth areas in a wholesale way. A growth area should be targeted for development only if you and your employee assess that there is real potential for improvement in this area and that the improvement will pay meaningful dividends.

7. FOLLOW-UP AND REINFORCEMENT ARE NECESSARY FOR SUCCESS

Oftentimes, typical performance development efforts don't involve adequate follow-up and reinforcement. This is most evident with training, in which employees are commonly sent to courses that seem to occur in a vacuum. Even if employees are energized and enlightened by these training courses, they typically go back to an organizational culture that causes them to revert to their old behavior because no reinforcement for that new behavior is built in to the company culture. No one is holding them accountable for using the new techniques, and, worse, employees are sometimes passively or actively discouraged by colleagues and superiors from doing things differently. Unfortunately, training classes often occur on a one-time basis, with no elements of follow-up or reinforcement.

For reinforcement and accountability to take place, the following three things must happen in the organization:

1. Top leaders in the department and/or organization need to "buy in" to the importance of spending time developing performance. This buy-in can be evidenced by leaders participating in the initial rollout of performance development efforts (attending, or even teaching, training in using a performance development model), providing additional resources, and/or consistently communicating and reinforcing the importance of performance development.

2. The use of a performance development model needs to be added to the list of key responsibilities in the job profile of every employee. This practice not only signals buy-in from the organization but also gives employees "permission" to spend some of their time on performance development. In addition, it provides leaders with a tool for holding employees accountable for developing their own performance.

3. Leaders must be held accountable by those above them in the management hierarchy for using the model to develop each employee, and then leaders should be rewarded when they are successful in developing employee performance.

If using the model on a regular basis is not part of an employee's or leader's job description—if it is seen as supplementary rather than essential—employees and leaders will have no strong incentive to use it. And the model, even if appreciated when initially taught, will fail to be followed if top leaders do not support (whether directly or indirectly) its use. To be effective, the model must be applied consistently and treated as an integral aspect of doing business at an organization. This can occur only if the organizational culture supports the model and its philosophy of performance development.

Where the Model Won't Help

For all the strengths and practical applications of the Exemplary Performance Model, it's still important to recognize areas where the model is not intended to be useful. These are:

- To correct negative employee conduct
- To correct extremely poor performance
- To help employees become exemplary in every area of performance
- To help people who don't want to be helped

NEGATIVE CONDUCT

First, the model is not meant to be helpful in dealing with severe or negative employee conduct. If you have an employee who fights, yells, threatens, or throws temper tantrums, for example, the Exemplary Performance Model does not provide tools to address this kind of poor conduct. The same would apply to an employee who steals clients, sells confidential information, intentionally breaks office equipment, or physically harms another employee: the present performance model is not going to help overcome this kind of extreme behavior. Instead, the model is meant to help leaders work with the majority of employees, who fall statistically in the midsection of a normal bell curve, as well as with those who fall at the right end of the bell curve, where performance is already exemplary. (See figure 2.)

EXTREMELY POOR PERFORMANCE

Second, the Exemplary Performance Model is not meant to be used to improve extremely poor performance, the kind that would cause you to fire someone: total inability to grasp concepts, nonexistent communication skills, or appalling customer service, for example. This may seem intuitive, but it is worth mentioning. In reality, you're not going to be saying in one breath, "How can you leverage your strengths?" and in the next breath, "By the way, you're fired." If someone has performed so poorly that you are strongly considering letting the person go, the Exemplary Performance Model is not going to help overcome this kind of performance. The model is not designed to help leaders

FIGURE 2 **Target Employees for Exemplary Performance Model**

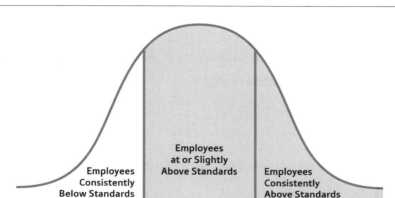

overcome gross inadequacies in employees, other than to help leaders note that employee talent and fit for a job are nonexistent across the board, in which case leaders will typically terminate employees or transfer them to a new job where talent and fit do exist. Again, the model is meant to help leaders work with the majority of employees, who fit in the midsection of a normal bell curve—as well as those on the right end.

EVERY AREA OF PERFORMANCE

Third, this model is not intended to help employees become exemplary in every single area of their performance. There are many tasks in a job that need to be accomplished, and in most cases, people won't be able to excel at every one of these tasks. For example, part of my current job responsibilities involves writing product requirement documents. Although I've learned to write these documents in an adequate manner—to meet organizational standards—I will never be an exemplary performer in this area. My strengths lie elsewhere, for example, with performance consulting and making presentations. This is fine, because the most important parts of my job—the parts that have the most impact on the company's bottom line—are the parts that I'm good at. There is no sense in my trying to reach the exemplary level for writing product requirement documents because I lack the potential to ever meet that goal.

Instead of aiming to help employees become exemplary at every task assigned to them—an unrealistic goal that may involve unneeded, excessive efforts, resources, and stress—the present model focuses on helping leaders raise employees to the exemplary level in *targeted areas* where (a) employees have already demonstrated some strength, and (b) the most impact on the company's execution of strategy will be realized. In particular, with the present model, you will pick only one growth area of performance to focus on at a time—the area you identify as having the most potential to yield positive results for the organization. In this way, you won't be wasting energy on helping the employee develop performance in areas that don't really matter.

THOSE REFUSING HELP

Finally, this model is not meant to help people who don't want to be helped—those who actively or passively refuse to participate in the development process. There are times when, for one reason or another, a person is content with where he is, and does not wish to change. Worse yet, there are a small number of people who purposely do just enough to get by. When this occurs, there is a deeper underlying cause that is beyond the scope of this model. Although the model does address performance issues that relate to motivation, the model can address motivation only at the "local" level. So the model is useful if an employee is unmotivated to engage in a certain task or key responsibility (the local level) but will not be effective if the employee has no larger motivation to reach an exemplary level of performance (global level) or to engage in the process of developing performance. The solution to a universally unmotivated employee is beyond the scope of the model. This lack of motivation is exhibited when someone refuses to self-assess, doesn't contribute to the creation of a development plan, and/or does not follow through on the development plan.

Conclusion

I have tested the Exemplary Performance Model in many real-life situations and have made several adjustments and improvements to it. In working with the model and teaching others about it, I have discovered that the model is easy enough to use, so that anyone can do it. But most of all, I have seen leaders get results when they engage this model. They are able to develop their employees' abilities and raise those employees' performance to new levels. They are able to meet and even exceed organizational goals. If you are a training and development professional, you will be able, after reading this book, to offer your leaders more than employee training as a way to develop employees; you will be able to open their eyes to a host of other options for developing performance, without the burden of long and expensive certifications. If you are a leader, you will finally understand why sending your people to training often doesn't improve performance. Better yet, you will have a variety of means for developing your employees, and you will know how to target their performance areas that will deliver the most punch.

2

The Exemplary Performance Model Explained

Unfortunately, there is no magic wand for improving employee performance. As leaders, we can't simply tell employees that we need them to get better at what they do and expect things to change. Corrective marks on an appraisal report aren't sufficient; yelling orders at employees won't yield significant improvements in perform-ance, either. Similarly, ignoring performance issues, as busy leaders are often tempted to do, will not have the desired effect of resolving them. While time may heal all wounds, time in and of itself does nothing to improve perfor-mance. Time will contribute to performance development only if leaders use their time wisely—to actively engage employees in an intentional and well-planned performance develop-ment process. The Exemplary Performance Model represents one such process.

Time will contribute to per-formance development only if leaders use their time wisely—to actively engage employees in an intentional and well-planned perfor-mance development process.

My goal in this chapter is to provide you with an overview of the Exemplary Performance Model so you can begin to understand the basics of how the model can be used. As I will explain in this chapter, the Exemplary Performance Model is based on four steps for developing performance. These steps revolve around a strengths-based focus, in which weaknesses are set aside and strengths become the focus of the development process. The model also provides leaders with a considerable range of tools for addressing performance areas so that leaders and employees have many options for creating a targeted and effective action plan for raising performance to the exemplary level. Finally, the model engages the leader and employee in a collaborative process, which strengthens the leader-employee relationship and further builds the employee's level of commitment to the performance development process. (Note that I intend in this chapter to give you a theoretical understanding of the model to lay the groundwork for understanding the performance factors I discuss in chapters 3–9, while I will examine in depth in chapter 10 how the model is practically applied.)

The Steps in the Model

There are four essential steps to using the Exemplary Performance Model.

THE FOUR STEPS IN THE EXEMPLARY PERFORMANCE MODEL

1. **Assess and target performance**—Identify an employee's strengths and weaknesses and select *one exemplary strength* (a task the employee engages in that yields exemplary results) and *one expandable strength* (a task that yields at-standards or greater results but less than exemplary results, and has the potential to become exemplary) to target; set weaknesses aside.

2. **Diagnose cause(s) of performance**—Determine the cause (key performance factor) yielding the high performance associated with the exemplary strength and the cause keeping the expandable strength from becoming an exemplary one.

3. **Develop and implement a plan**—Develop an action plan that applies the right tool(s) to *leverage* the exemplary strength (transfer it to others) and the right tool(s) to *develop* the expandable strength; then work with the employee to implement the plan.

4. **Follow up**—Follow up to see how the performance development process is working to leverage and develop the targeted strengths, and adjust the action plan if needed.

Although there are additional layers to the Exemplary Performance Model, the above description conveys the overall strategy of the model in an easily digestible package.

Development as an Iterative and Parallel Process

In figure 3 on the following page, the exemplary performance process is shown in its true form, as a "cycle." The process is intended to be iterative: repeated again and again to develop multiple areas of performance to the exemplary level (and to leverage multiple exemplary strengths). Once follow-up reveals that the targeted performance area has been leveraged to satisfaction (for exemplary strengths) or developed to an exemplary level (for expandable strengths), the leader and employee should begin the development cycle again, targeting a new expandable strength to raise to the exemplary level or targeting a different exemplary strength to leverage for other employees' benefit.

Because the Exemplary Performance Model involves targeting one exemplary strength and one expandable strength at any given time, you will actually engage in a series of parallel steps when using the model.

As you move through each step of the model, you will perform that step for both an exemplary strength and an expandable strength. The speed at which you and an employee successfully leverage an exemplary strength and develop the employee's expandable strength may, of course, vary. You will not always be on the same numbered

FIGURE 3   **Exemplary Performance Development Cycle**

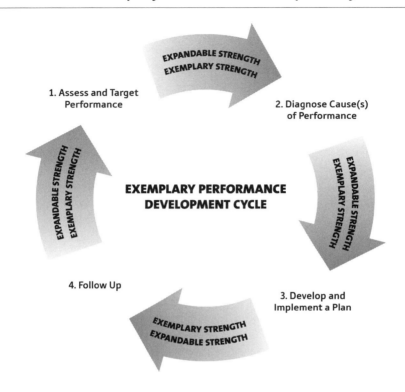

step for each strength as you work your way through the development process. In the first round of using the model, you may proceed simultaneously for each of the two targeted strengths through steps 1 to 3, but when you get to step 4 (follow-up), you well may take longer to work through this step for one of the targeted strengths than for the other.

How the Model Defines Strengths and Weaknesses

The first part of the model involves differentiating between an employee's strengths and weaknesses. To do this, it is important to know how the model defines strength and weakness.

STRENGTHS

When I mentioned earlier that there are two kinds of strengths targeted in this model, you may have paused and wondered how that could be. Isn't a strength a strength? Most of us tend to think of a strength simply as something that a person is good at doing; we juxtapose strength to weakness, something that someone is not good at doing. So strengths are one thing, and weaknesses are the opposite. Does this mean, however, that there can't be more than one kind of strength? No, it doesn't. If we push a little further, most of us would agree that any one person probably has strengths of varying degrees—things the person does well, things the person does even better, and things the person does at an exemplary level. For example, I might be good at singing, even better at playing the guitar, and excellent at writing songs. So, I have three different strengths, with one of these being exemplary (songwriting) and the others being expandable (good but possibly with room for growth to the exemplary level).

Although strengths occur on a spectrum from good to better to best, for the purposes of this model, I group them into just two categories: expandable and exemplary.

Exemplary Strengths
These are those areas of performance (at the task level) that yield sustained exemplary results—those that *consistently* match the performance of exemplars in the field or industry. This definition is similar to Marcus Buckingham and Donald Clifton's definition of *strength*: an area where someone performs consistently at near perfect levels.[1]

Expandable Strengths
Expandable strengths are those areas of performance (at the task level) that yield results that are less than exemplary but meet organizational standards or slightly exceed them—and have the potential to be developed at or near the exemplary level. This potential is an important component of expandable strengths because it helps you identify areas for which investment in performance development will likely yield significant results. You don't want to focus on performance areas where an employee is meeting standards but doesn't evince the potential to increase performance much beyond those standards, because

A PARADIGM SHIFT

Only recently has the field of HR, learning, and organization development recognized the value of focusing on strengths for development. Slowly, professionals are starting to recognize the practical value of research[2] revealing that targeting strengths for development provides more significant improvements in performance than targeting weaknesses. Even more slowly, this philosophy is filtering down to line managers. Thus, when you introduce the idea to your leaders of setting weaknesses aside when developing performance, you may hear some grumbling, resistance, or challenge. Certainly, you want to acknowledge the importance of raising someone's weaknesses in performance in critical areas of his job to the at-standards level during the performance management process, but take this opportunity to inform leaders about the potential of a strengths-focused performance development process to yield exemplary performance—something every leader can get excited about.

you won't get much reward for your time and effort to develop that performance.

WEAKNESSES

Weaknesses are those areas of performance (at the task level) that yield results that are consistently below organizational standards. It is uncommon for a person to be able to develop his or her weaknesses to the exemplary level, so once you identify weaknesses, you will set them aside when using this model rather than target them. If weaknesses occur in critical areas of a person's job, you will need to address these in the performance *management* process. The performance development process focuses specifically on the growth and improvement of performance, while the performance management process focuses on rating performance for all responsibilities and on documenting it annually.

Developing Versus Leveraging a Strength

As you may have noticed in the earlier overview of the steps in the performance model, I used the word *leveraging* rather than *developing* to refer to the way you will be addressing an employee's exemplary strength. I purposely do not use the term *develop* because the process of targeting the exemplary strength is quite different from that of targeting the expandable strength. For expandable strengths, you truly are trying to increase performance from the at-standards level to the exemplary level, so *develop* is the appropriate term. In contrast, for exemplary strengths, the primary goal is not to increase the employee's performance; it is to learn from that employee's strengths and to apply that new knowledge to increase the performance of others in the department. When and where possible, you will try to *leverage, or transfer,* an employee's exemplary strength to other employees. What I mean by leveraging someone's exemplary performance, then, is that you will identify the primary cause (factor) for that performance (e.g., skills and knowledge, tools and resources, systems and processes, etc.) and then create an action plan that capitalizes on that identification to increase the performance of others to (or near) the exemplary level for that same task.

Leveraging an employee's exemplary strength can occur in a variety of forms. For example, you might create an action plan to:

- Share the employee's expertise with the rest of the team through training or mentoring led by that employee
- Provide tools to the other employees that the exemplary employee is already using
- Alter a departmental process to include an innovation developed by the exemplary employee

There are three side benefits of leveraging exemplary strengths, beyond transferring the exemplary strength to other employees. First, you will likely motivate and energize the employee to stay engaged in the development process by allowing him or her to share an exemplary strength for the betterment of the whole department and by recognizing the employee for being an expert at that particular task. Second, you may inadvertently help your employee improve his or her strength from the exemplary level to the cutting-edge level. That is, during the process of focusing on the exemplary strength, you might develop a totally new way of doing something that yields results beyond anything previously attained. Third, by leveraging exemplary strengths, you will have a more comprehensive method of developing exemplary performance than if you focus on expandable strengths alone. A whole new avenue for raising employee performance will be at your disposal when you involve exemplary employees in the performance development process of others, rather than, as the leader, retaining performance development exclusively in your domain.

An additional benefit of leveraging exemplary strengths is that as you identify exemplary strengths among different employees in your organization, you will gain valuable insight into how you can potentially alter roles to play on these individuals' strengths and to reduce the effect of others' weaknesses in the same performance area. The highest-performing teams are not those in which every person is good at everything but those groups whose leaders have learned to leverage everyone's strengths and to minimize the effects of everyone's weaknesses (by altering roles, hiring talent to fill in for weaknesses, etc.).

Steps of the Model

Now that the key terms of the model have been defined, let's look more closely at each of the four steps in the model.

STEP 1: ASSESSING AND TARGETING CURRENT PERFORMANCE

Step 1 of the Exemplary Performance Model is to determine which two strengths (one exemplary, one expandable) you and your employee would like to target during the first cycle of the performance development process. To make this decision, you will first need to identify the employee's strengths and weaknesses. Once you have accomplished this task, you will set weaknesses aside and sort strengths into two groups: exemplary and expandable. Next, you can move on to identifying which one exemplary strength and which one expandable strength you want to target during this cycle of performance development. (If no exemplary strength exists, select two expandable strengths.) During this phase of step 1, the goal is to identify which strengths will yield the most benefit when addressed—which will provide the most "bang for the buck." In other words, you will select the target strengths on the basis of which ones are expected to have the greatest business impact.

STEP 2: DETERMINING THE CAUSE FOR CURRENT PERFORMANCE

Once you've identified which two strengths you and the employee would like to target, you are ready to roll up your sleeves and do some digging. It's time to identify the key performance factor related to that strength.

For exemplary strengths, you will be interested in determining which performance factor is most responsible for driving the employee's ability to perform at an exemplary level. Certainly, multiple performance factors will be working together to help the employee be successful, but your goal will be to determine which factor is predominant—which factor seems to point most clearly to the difference between exemplary performance by this employee and at-standards performance by other employees.

For expandable strengths, you will be interested in determining which performance factor most explains the gap between the current performance level and the exemplary level. In other words, which performance factor needs to be primarily addressed to move performance to the exemplary level?

In the case of either strength type (exemplary or expandable), identifying the key performance factor will help you understand why the person performs the targeted task (strength) at the given level. Subsequently, that knowledge will help you create a targeted action plan in step 3. But first, let's examine the different performance factors you will be considering in step 2 of the model.

THE PERFORMANCE FACTORS

The Exemplary Performance Model, building on predecessor models, provides seven possible factors (see figure 4) that may lie at the heart of a targeted strength. These factors are talent and fit, environment,

FIGURE 4   **The Seven Performance Factors**

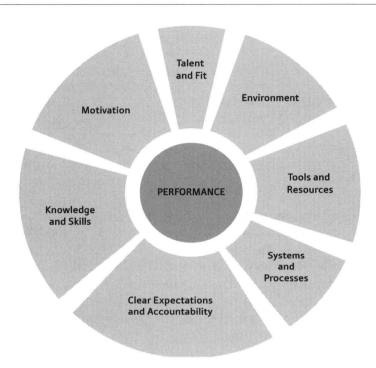

tools and resources, systems and processes, clear expectations and ac-countability, knowledge and skills, and motivation.

Table 1 provides a description of each of these seven performance factors.

Here are a few examples of how a given performance factor may be the cause of a particular exemplary or expandable strength.

- A retail employee is excellent (exemplary) at decorating the storefront window display because she has taken an interior design course that other employees have not taken (knowledge and skills).

- A home inspector has demonstrated the potential to achieve exemplary performance at writing up inspection reports (expandable strength) but has not yet consistently achieved the

TABLE 1 **The Seven Performance Factors Defined**

FACTOR	DEFINITION
Talent and fit	The combination of innate abilities that give people the potential to excel at a given task (talent); the alignment of personal preferences with the work group norms, requirements, and practices (fit)
Environment	The physical, emotional, and interpersonal elements that make up the atmosphere in which people work (work environment) and live (personal environment)
Tools and resources	The equipment, information, and support people use to achieve desired outcomes
Systems and processes	The interaction among variables that all work together to achieve outcomes (systems); and the specific steps people engage in to achieve results for a specific task (processes)
Clear expectations and accountability	Communications and interactions that help people understand specifically what is expected of them (clear expectations); communications, interactions, and consequences that hold people responsible for achieving outcomes (accountability)
Knowledge and skills	The expertise and education people need in order to achieve outcomes (knowledge); the developed ability to perform tasks and achieve out-comes (skills)
Motivation	The drive or desire people have to achieve results

exemplary level because the rewards for writing an exemplary report are insufficient to motivate him (motivation factor).

- A sous-chef at a four-star restaurant makes exemplary Cobb salad because he cooks the bacon for one minute less than the other sous-chefs do (a deviation from the standard process; system and processes factor).

You will learn more about the characteristics of each performance factor, and how to determine whether that factor is at play in a given performance issue, as you read chapters 3–9. For now, table 1 provides a basic understanding of the nature of each factor and how each relates to performance so you can better understand step 2 of the model. Once you are familiar with the factors, you will have the information you need to develop a specific action plan for developing or leveraging the targeted strengths, which takes place in step 3. (You will gain more insight into how to determine which performance factor is primarily at play in a targeted strength as you read through the rest of the book.)

STEP 3: CREATING AN ACTION PLAN

Once you and your employee have targeted an exemplary and an expandable strength (step 1) and identified the key performance factor relevant to the targeted strength (step 2), you are ready to create an action plan for developing and leveraging the targeted areas of performance. The factor you select for each strength in step 2 will help you determine which tools to build into the action plan.

Figure 5 shows the seven factors with the tools that can typically be applied to address each factor. For example, if you've identified that lack of skills and knowledge is at the root of an employee's mistakes while entering data, you can look at the outer ring of the model that is attached to the knowledge and skills factor and incorporate one or more of the associated tools—for example, training, role modeling, or observation—into your action plan. Alternatively, if you've identified lack of motivation as the reason an employee makes mistakes while entering data, you can look at the outer ring of tools attached to the motivation factor and consider building an action plan that entails giving the employee more challenging assignments or creating an environment in which the employee feels empowered.

Your action plan should include specific, measurable goals; who is responsible for accomplishing each goal; and when these goals should be completed. Sometimes, both the leader and the employee will be responsible for items in the action plan; at other times, only the employee will be responsible (e.g., taking a training class, printing and using a job aid, seeking assistance from a qualified counselor); and at still other times, the leader alone will be responsible for items on the

FIGURE 5   **Tools of the Exemplary Performance Model**

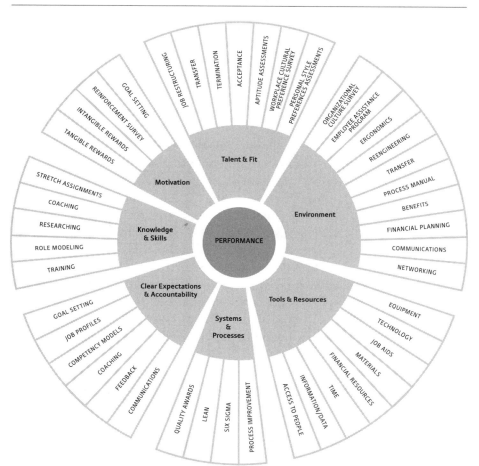

action plan (e.g., redesigning an ineffective process, supplying needed equipment). In chapter 10, I will provide more detailed guidance on creating an action plan.

Although the Exemplary Performance Model provides a multitude of tools for addressing any given performance factor, these tools are not intended to be all-encompassing. In addition to being free to use tools other than those shown in the Exemplary Performance Model (figure 5), you can also borrow a tool associated with one particular factor to address another factor. For example, you might borrow the coaching tool from the knowledge and skills factor and use it to help leverage an exemplary strength that is driven primarily by talent and fit. Although coaching is shown in the model as a tool for addressing skills-and-knowledge-related performance issues, coaching can also help you leverage exemplary strengths that have root causes other than knowledge and skills.

STEP 4: FOLLOWING UP

During step 4 of the performance development process, follow-up, you and the employee assess current progress toward completing the action plan and identify which roadblocks, if any, have arisen. If roadblocks are detected, a number of tactics can be used. For example, you and the employee can break down the action plan into the exact steps needed to achieve its specific goals. The employee can be encouraged to indicate what additional or new support she needs to be successful. And the two of you may need to add new tools or action items to the action plan (e.g., doing some research to learn more about a topic, or updating the employee's job profile to set clearer expectations). You may also need to revisit steps 2 and 3 of the model to determine whether the right factor was initially chosen and then adjust the action plan if necessary.

Check-in meetings at step 4 of the process can yield a variety of results. Depending on the particular targeted task, action plan, and time frame, you might find that you and/or the employee have completed a few steps on the action plan, no steps, or all of the steps. For a variety of reasons, you might both be making progress, might both be stuck, or might have jointly completed the action plan. (If the last of these, you and the employee will be ready to return to step 1 of the exemplary performance development cycle and select a new strength to leverage or develop.) Step 4 of the model is unique and customized.

Unfortunately, this fourth step of the model is often overlooked by leaders involved in developing their employees. As I have seen time and again, many organizations and organizational leaders fail to close the circle of performance development: they set their employees up with training or resources or solutions intended to increase performance (step 3) but then don't check in to see how things are going.

Yet, if employees are not engaged by their leaders to evaluate how the performance development process is going, they will take this as a

> ## WHAT'S THE DIFFERENCE BETWEEN
> ## A JOB DESCRIPTION AND A JOB PROFILE?
>
> A job description typically lists a short description of the job, along with the key responsibilities, education level, and experience needed for that job. A job profile expands on the job description to also include tasks, knowledge, skills, abilities, and behaviors required for success in that job. Ideally, a job profile will also detail the level of performance needed (the standard and metric) for each key responsibility and, when possible, for each task. If you do not currently have job profiles on record for your employees' jobs, you will need to create the requisite job profiles before you can use the Exemplary Performance Model effectively. Developing a job profile is a relatively straightforward process, but it nonetheless involves many steps. To learn more about creating effective job profiles, you can check the latest book offerings from the American Society for Training and Development as well as from the Society for Human Resource Management.

sign from their leaders that the development process is not valued. Employees will assign much higher priority to other key responsibilities and tasks on their to-do lists, and the process of developing performance will fall to the bottom of the list, if not disappear altogether.

Furthermore, performance development is necessarily collaborative. The leader will have an important perspective on how the process is going and can work with the employee to tweak the action plan, if needed. The exemplary performance development effort is, through and through, a collaborative process to which both the employee and the leader are essential.

Building the Right Infrastructure

Before you can successfully use the Exemplary Performance Model, there are certain key elements or prerequisites that must be in place. For example, a job profile is an essential prerequisite to enacting step 1 of the model (assessing employee performance). That is, you can't assess someone's performance unless you have a comprehensive list of

TABLE 2 **Prerequisites for Using the Exemplary Performance Model**

PREREQUISITE	EXPLANATION
Job profile	The job profile provides the necessary standards and metrics for assessing current employee performance (step 1 of the model).
Good communication and a trusting relationship	Because the Exemplary Performance Model relies on a collaborative process between employee and leader, the two must have a trusting relationship that enables clear, candid, effective communication.
Employee desire to improve	If the employee has no interest in getting better at his or her job, or the employee simply does not believe that the model will be effective, this underlying lack of motivation will sabotage any results that the model might potentially yield. (See "Where the Model Won't Help" in chapter 1.)
Employee ability to self-assess	Employee input is an essential part of the collaborative development process between leader and employee. To be an effective member of the team, the employee must have the ability to accurately diagnose where his performance is strong and where his performance could improve.
Organizational buy-in	No matter how much a leader coaches the employee to develop performance, if the rest of the company does not value the performance development process, the employee will receive signals everywhere that he should not spend time and energy developing performance. This message will substantially limit the effectiveness of the model.

the key responsibilities, tasks, knowledge, skills, and abilities required in that person's work. The job profile provides such a detailed list.

In this chapter I will not go deeply into how to develop these prerequisite elements, but I will provide a comprehensive checklist on what these elements are so you can assess whether you are ready to begin using the model or whether you instead need to invest time building the right performance development infrastructure at your organization. Table 2 contains an overview of the prerequisites needed for using the model.

As for the issue of fostering organizational buy-in, I offer the following suggestions.

Add the use of the Exemplary Performance Model to the job profile for each employee in your department. By adding the use of the model to the employee's list of key responsibilities, you are signaling its importance to the employee, giving her permission to engage with this model, and letting her know it is important to give this key responsibility time and attention. You are informing the employee that she is responsible for using the Exemplary Performance Model to develop her performance and indicating that she will be evaluated in the use of the model.

Senior leaders can also communicate their interest in employees' using this model by co-teaching it with the department leader. When employees see one of the organization's senior leaders teaching the model, they will know it is truly valued by the leader and the organization.

Interestingly, it has not been challenging for me to get clients to buy in to the use of the Exemplary Performance Model because most people can see that it has great potential to work, especially when I share with them stories of the many successes I've encountered or observed over the years. This "face validity" of the model might make it easier for you to get support throughout your organization. If you do encounter naysayers, though, try not to be discouraged. When critics see the positive results of using the model, they might just come around to seeing its value.

Conclusion

As you begin getting comfortable with using the Exemplary Performance Model, feel free to let your employees know that you, like them, are in the process of learning the model and that you might make mistakes along the way. Most employees will appreciate your candor and will gain from this shared honesty a willingness to make mistakes themselves (to "fail forward")[3] as well as an increased ability to communicate honestly with you. In addition, try not to sweat the small stuff; if you feel after the fact that you've targeted the wrong strength—for example, one that won't have the most return on investment—remember that you're still helping to develop the individual (in the case of the expandable strength) or to share a valuable strength with other employees (in the case of the exemplary strength), and there's no harm in that process. The next time you return to step 1 of the model, you can focus on finding a strength that will have a greater impact.

Once the model becomes familiar to you, you will actually start to think in terms of the seven factors and will be able to help people get at the root of how to improve performance or leverage a strength without having the model in front of you. More importantly, you will be able to ask the right questions to guide people through a self-assessment process in which they come up with the answers themselves. Such a process can be very motivating to individuals and will often lead them to want to reach exemplary performance.

Part 2

The Exemplary Performance Factors

3

The Talent and Fit Factor

Have you ever had an employee who was a real pleasure to be around but who was terrible at his job—such as the really friendly third-stringer on the football team who cracks great jokes but can't catch a ball to save his life? Have you ever felt stuck with an employee—as if you or your predecessor made the wrong hiring decision and now you have to live with the person, pulling out your hair because attempts to improve performance always end up falling flat? Sometimes, no matter how likable or hardworking an employee is or how much effort you together invest in improving her performance, reality dictates that she will never be good at her current job. She will never be good, not because she isn't motivated, or because she doesn't have the tools she needs to do her job, but because she simply doesn't have the talent or fit for the job.

The talent and fit factor refers to that seemingly intangible area of performance that pegs to a person's natural abilities and preferences.

The talent and fit factor refers to that intangible area of performance that pegs to a person's natural abilities and preferences. It refers

TALENT AND FIT: A DIFFERENT FACTOR

The talent and fit factor is different in several ways from any of the other factors in the Exemplary Performance Model:

• Talent and fit are required to achieve exemplary performance.

• Talent and fit can be assessed and measured—but not changed or improved.

• You cannot develop an expandable strength with the tools from the talent and fit factor; you can develop an expandable strength only with tools from other factors.

to a person's gifts and passions and to whether those gifts and passions are suited to the key responsibilities, skills, and competencies required for a given job. Interestingly, although the talent and fit factor can be assessed and measured, it can't be changed. In this way, the talent and fit factor is unique among all the performance factors. While the other six performance factors can actually be altered, talent and fit cannot. It is important to note that talent is necessary for achieving exemplary performance; without talent, a person may be able to meet organizational standards for a task, but she will not be able to engage in that task at the exemplary level.[1]

Talent and Fit Defined

The talent and fit factor is made up of two components, both are similar in that they refer to innate, unchangeable aspects of a person. Let's look at the definitions of each of these components.

▪ *Talent* refers to the combination of innate abilities that give people the potential to excel at a given task.

▪ *Fit* refers to the alignment of personal preferences with the work group norms, requirements, and practices.

Although you can teach your employees new skills and knowledge, connect them with tools and resources, make adjustments to increase their motivation, improve their work environment, set clearer expectations, and improve work processes (six of the seven performance factors), you cannot take measures to increase an employee's talent or fit. There are certainly some things you can do to address talent and fit issues, but if a person lacks talent or fit for a job as a whole or for the critical areas of that job (rather than for only certain less critical tasks in that job), you may be faced with the difficult choice of realigning the person into another position or letting him go. Thus, it's ideal to assess talent and fit at the hiring stage.

Talent

To review, talent is the combination of innate abilities that gives people the potential to excel at a given task. Another way of describing talent is as an intrinsic aptitude for fulfilling a certain behavior, set of behaviors, or tasks—an aptitude that gives someone the potential to perform at an exemplary level. Talent is a result of:

- Physical makeup
- Brain function
- Personality characteristics

Table 3 on the following page describes the three components of talent and provides examples so you can see how each of these components contributes to talent in the real world.

When we look at the three components of talent—physical makeup, brain function, and personality characteristics—we can see that these things are more or less fixed by the time someone enters the workforce. Physical traits are largely unchangeable; core brain development is complete by adulthood; and personality characteristics—though they can be affected by ongoing life experience, self-discovery, or even counseling—are not something you will be able to alter in a meaningful way in the work setting. So the talent that someone brings to the workplace is not something that can be "taught" at work. This is why I call talent unchangeable: people either have talent for something or they do not.

Yes, skills in areas where people have talent can be increased—for example, through training and practice that provide someone with the practical skills needed to *apply* his or her talent—but training and prac-

TABLE 3 **What Makes Up Talent?**

TALENT COMPONENT	DESCRIPTION	REAL-WORLD EXAMPLE
Physical makeup	A person's physical traits, including things such as one's body type, physical dexterity, voice quality, and eyesight	Elisa is 6'2" with a muscular build and great physical coordination and dexterity, which suits her to play basketball.
Brain function	A person's neural aptitudes for certain subjects (e.g., math, art, communications)	Joe's brain is "wired" for strategic thinking, which makes him talented at chess, a game based on thinking several moves ahead.
Personality characteristics	A person's attributes for understanding and acting in the world (friendly or shy, optimistic or pessimistic, talkative or quiet)	Pat was raised in a home with an alcoholic parent, which taught her to be guarded and suspicious of people in relationships. Her personality characteristic of being guarded and suspicious of people makes her difficult to get along with.

tice cannot *create* talent out of thin air. Take world-famous former basketball star Michael Jordan as an example. During his years as a professional basketball player for the Chicago Bulls, Jordan's disciplined approach to training (for example, adding a morning workout before the required 9:00–11:00 workout during the regular season) undoubtedly enhanced his natural talent. As Chad Zimmerman noted in *Stack*, "The training took Jordan beyond what any player, past or present, has ever accomplished. Critics went from 'Can he do that?' to 'How did he do that?'"[2] By sharpening his skills and keeping his body in top physical form, Jordan was able to capitalize on his athletic talent and achieve exemplary performance. Yet most people would not contend that Jordan became an NBA legend solely because of his training regimen; instead, they would acknowledge that Jordan had an innate talent for basketball that, in conjunction with his hard work and determination, propelled him to breaking records and to leading the Chicago Bulls to six national championships.

Similarly, most people who have seen me play basketball would recognize that even if I took up the exact training routine of Michael Jordan during his glory days and came under the tutelage of his former coach, Phil Jackson, I would never come close to achieving Jordan's degree of performance in the game. While practice and training are usually necessary for achieving exemplary performance in basketball or any other field and can lead to the development of *skills,* practice and training alone are not usually sufficient for exemplary performance; talent is necessary too. Ultimately, skills and talent are *both* necessary for exemplary performance; skills can supplement existing talent or can allow a hidden talent to become visible.

Fit

As I mentioned earlier, fit refers to the alignment of personal preferences with work group norms, requirements, and practices. In other words, fit is the degree to which a person naturally conforms to and feels comfortable with her job responsibilities and work setting.

Two elements make up fit:

- Passion

- Preferences

Note that fit cannot be faked. A person might be able to force himself out of a comfort zone for a period of time, but passion and preferences cannot be faked for an extended period. A person's "true colors" will eventually reveal themselves, or the person will choose to leave a job in pursuit of something that better matches his passion and preferences. Anyone who's been put in a sales job who dislikes the idea of "pushing" a product or anyone who loves spending time with others but ends up in a job where human interaction is limited knows what it means to have poor fit with a job. An ill-fitted salesperson can pick up the phone and make cold calls or a gregarious person can sit at a desk in silence all day, but neither will enjoy his or her work, and this will likely evidence itself in performance over time. Further, the ill-fitted person will likely be motivated to look for a new job that is better suited to his or her preferences.

PASSION

Passion refers to a person's innate desire to engage in a certain kind of work. For example, I love developing people's performance; it brings me pleasure to help others in this way, and I am fascinated by the topic. So I read literature on performance development, I have a job that involves a lot of key responsibilities regarding performance development, I teach seminars on performance development, and I have written this book. My passion for performance development helps me to be successful at my job as vice president of talent management because I continually seek out opportunities to learn the emerging and world-class practices being incorporated at leading organizations. If I did not have this passion for performance development, I would not stay current on emerging practices, techniques, and research and would not be good in a role that required me to improve the performance of others or to teach others how to improve people's performance. Further, I would not enjoy my job and would not be driven to perform above expectations. Moreover, if I did not have a passion for performance development, no one could give me this passion or teach it to me. As with talent, people either have a passion for a certain subject or they don't.

PREFERENCES

Preferences, someone's innate combination of interests, compose the other aspect of fit. Preferences are similar to passion in that both involve a person's interest, but whereas passion applies to one's interest in a whole field, preferences refer to the specific setting, tasks, and key responsibilities that a person enjoys engaging in. For example, for a salesperson to have the right fit for her job, he or she needs to have preferences that align with the tasks, skills, and abilities in the job profile for that sales work—things such as a desire to spend time talking to others, a comfort level with discussing the attributes of a given product or service, and a willingness to encourage people to purchase a product or service. If a person does not have preferences for these activities, he or she will not be a good fit for a sales job.

WHEN LACK OF FIT IS THE "FALL GUY"

Lack of fit can sometimes be used as an excuse for less-than-exemplary employee performance ("This person just doesn't fit in here") by leaders who don't know how to determine the root causes of performance when, in reality, performance is suffering because of some other reason that can actually be addressed. You can avoid this pitfall by examining each of the factors when assessing the root cause of performance rather than looking only at the talent and fit factor.

Preference categories can include:

- How a person works best (alone or in groups)
- The kind of interaction a person prefers (casual versus formal)
- A person's desired work mode for handling projects (multitasking versus focusing)
- The speed at which a person likes to work (quickly or slowly)

There are several preference models that can help you assess a person's preferences at work. These include the Work Preferences Inventory (available at http://www.careerperfect.com/content/career-planning-work-preference-inventory) and the Work Preferences Questionnaire (available at http://www.greatbiztools.com), to name two. Familiarizing yourself with one or more of these models will facilitate your ability to assess a person's fit for a job or for tasks within that job.

How Much Talent and Fit Is Enough?

People have varying degrees of talent and fit for the different aspects of a given job. They will be more talented for and better suited to certain parts of their jobs than other parts. For example, your administrative assistant may have a real talent for managing your schedule, while she is less talented at setting up for meetings.

If you discover that talent or fit is lacking for a targeted performance area, this does not necessarily mean that you must transition the person into another role or let him go. Instead, you may decide that you can help the employee compensate for a lack of talent by increasing certain skills or enlisting the help of a colleague, or you can make changes to his key responsibilities (see more in "Tools to Compensate for Lack of Talent or Fit" below).

Yet it's important to recognize the reality that a person with little talent in an area will probably never become exemplary in that area, no matter what tools you use to address it. Instead, the person most likely has the potential only to become sufficient at meeting the requirements for a given job. If the lack of talent occurs in a relatively insignificant area of a job, this may be acceptable and something that can be adequately dealt with or accepted. If you discover that a person lacks talent or fit in a critical area of his job, however, you will need either someone else to compensate for that lack of talent and fit (take on affected responsibilities) or someone who does have the necessary talent and fit to replace the employee (again, I will discuss more about how to deal with this lack of talent or fit later in the chapter).

Ultimately, you want to aim to hire employees who have talent and fit for the critical areas of their jobs so that they have the potential to reach exemplary performance in these areas, since this is ideal for organizational productivity and strategic execution. Talent and fit are less necessary in less critical areas of someone's job, where at-standards performance may be all that's required for successful completion of a task, or where no significant gains in productivity and strategic execution will be realized by achieving exemplary performance.

Is the Talent and Fit Factor Key to an Expandable Strength?

When assessing whether the talent and fit factor is the primary reason why performance is not at an exemplary level, you will find it helpful to ask the following questions:

1. Does the person exhibit the physical traits, intellectual ability, and personality characteristics (the talent) needed to be successful at this type of task?

2. Does the person display passion and preference (fit) for working on this type of task?

3. Does the person display passion and preference (fit) for the organizational culture and values?

ASSESSING TALENT AND FIT WHEN HIRING

In a perfect world, you will assess whether an individual has the talent and fit required for a job *before* hiring her. Ideal tools for making this assessment at the hiring stage include aptitude assessments, workplace cultural preferences surveys, and personal style preferences assessments.

- **Aptitude assessments** are tests that determine whether or not one has the natural ability to learn and perform specific tasks. They are used to measure such things as numerical and verbal aptitudes, spatial perception, and job-related perception. Examples include the *General Aptitude Test Battery* (GATB) and the *Wonderlic Personnel Test*.

- **Workplace cultural preferences surveys** examine what type of setting and environment a person likes to work in. When used as a survey, these instruments are usually administered throughout the workforce as a way to gauge the perceptions of specific cultural factors (such as leadership effectiveness, perceptions of benefits, opportunities for advancement, etc.). When used in hiring and/or promotion, questions to determine work culture preferences are included in interviews.

- **Personal style preferences assessments** refer to instruments such as the *Social Style Model* and the DISC. Additional tools include custom surveys that are created to measure one's preferences for the specific characteristics of the organization's culture.

Since talent and fit are prerequisites for achieving exemplary performance, it is ideal to assess talent and fit at the hiring stage. Nonetheless, if an employee slips through and is hired in spite of a lack of talent or fit, you can use the tools mentioned in this chapter to address the performance issue.

DOES THE PERSON EXHIBIT
THE TALENT FOR THIS TASK?

This process of assessing talent can be subjective as well as biased, so you want to proceed with care. To avoid unfair bias, you, as the leader, want to assess only those areas of physical traits, intellectual function, and personality characteristics that have been spelled out as necessary for a given job by the organizational policies and/or job profile (as opposed to generating your own subjective list). For example, if you are in the air force and are assessing someone's performance as a fighter pilot, it might be appropriate to look at the physical trait of eyesight by administering an eye test to the person, since twenty-twenty vision is needed for exemplary performance and is spelled out as a requirement in the job profile.

In contrast, if you are assessing a clerk in the mailroom for performance, you would not randomly refer the employee to have an eye test to measure the physical trait of eyesight unless (a) the job profile specifically indicated a requirement of twenty-twenty corrected vision, or (b) the employee assessed himself as having difficulty reading the mail when sorting envelopes for delivery. (Note that you would want to test the vision of prospective employees only after at least a conditional job offer has been made to avoid violating the Americans with Disabilities Act [ADA]. This timing would help you avoid unfair bias or subjectivity that could lead to legal action. Seek the advice of a qualified attorney for guidance on this topic.)

The previous paragraph refers mainly to physical traits, but what about brain function and personality characteristics? As for brain function, it's important to consider a few things. First, you are interested here, not in whether the person is intelligent but in whether the person's brain is "wired" in a way that allows him or her to be successful at the *specific, targeted task*. The type of test used to evaluate this kind of brain function is called a cognitive ability test. You will use these types of tests to get at the issue of whether the person has a potential for effectively engaging in this particular task (e.g., computing formulas, developing advertising slogans, learning languages) on the basis of cognitive strengths. Examples of cognitive ability tests include the *Wonderlic Personnel Test* and the *General Aptitude Test Battery* (GATB). Another easy way to gain information on brain function for a given task is to observe the employee when he or she is engaging in the task and to ask him or her to self-assess. Does the employee appear (or admit to being) confused or lost when engaged in the task? Does the employee say things such as "This just doesn't make sense to me" when trying to engage in the task? (Note that this statement could also point to a process issue.) When self-assessing, does the employee say things such as "I'm just not a natural at this sort of thing"? These are cues that the person's brain may not be wired in a way that allows exemplary performance in this area. Conversely, if brain function leads to an *exemplary* strength, the employee might make statements such as "That comes easily to me," "This just makes sense," or "I love doing X."

Personality tests, such as the *Minnesota Multiphasic Personality Inventory* (MMPI), the *Thematic Apperception Test* (TAT), and the *16 Personality Factors* (16PF), can be used to assess whether someone has the personality characteristics (e.g., conscientiousness, agreeableness, and openness to change) to perform well at a job. However, there are significant challenges to using personality tests. First, the use of these tests in selecting employees has been increasingly challenged in the courts owing to the difficulty of linking them directly to job duties. Second, there is a concern that individuals can gain the ability to learn what these personality tests are asking for (i.e., catch on to what's being measured) and provide the results that will put them in the most favorable light. Some tests try to combat this form of cheating by using a lie scale within the test.[3]

How, then, can assessing personality characteristics be applied to working with the Exemplary Performance Model? We can walk through an example to see. Let's say you are working with one of your agency's social workers to develop his performance, and you decide to target his exemplary strength of retaining 95 percent or more of the participants enrolled in his group therapy programs for the duration of the program. You may note that client survey feedback cites the employee's capacity to provide empathy (a personality characteristic) as one of the top three reasons clients stayed in therapy. You have data to show that the employee's capacity for empathy was relevant to his exemplary performance. To leverage this strength with other employees, you might then decide to have the employee conduct an in-service workshop for fellow employees on the outward behaviors he uses to convey empathy to clients (eye contact, appropriate listening noises, etc.). Although the employee won't be able to teach his colleagues to have a *talent* for empathy, he may be able to help them acquire empathic *skills* that improve their performance. Therefore, discovering the talent that drives exemplary performance may help you discover the skills needed to excel at a given key responsibility or task.

As you can imagine, no one likes to be told that there is something "wrong" with his personality, and that is in no way the goal here when addressing expandable strengths. To avoid this pitfall, try to focus on the fact that, as with brain function, you are not looking at someone's personality as a whole but rather at how a specific personality characteristic contributes to or detracts from the employee's ability to perform a *specific, targeted task*. Getting employees to self-assess—to share their own opinions on how their personality characteristics contribute to the performance of a given task—will go a long way toward avoiding making employees feel labeled or judged. Also, with personality characteristics as with strengths and weaknesses in step 1, it is natural to have greater talents at certain tasks than others. After all, you can't be great at everything.

DOES THE PERSON DISPLAY FIT FOR THE TASK?

The second question asks whether the person displays the passion and preferences necessary to excel at a specific task. We will examine each component separately.

Passion

When it comes to assessing someone's passion for a job, keep in mind that not everyone displays passion in the same way. Some people show their passion by verbally expressing excitement and interest in a job; others exhibit their passion by enthusiastically committing long hours to a project. Still others reveal their passion through the extra, unsolicited efforts they put into their work (like doing outside reading, research, or training) or by initiating new projects at work that relate to their passion. There is no test you can give to measure an employee's passion; instead, you will need to observe a person's behavior to see if it reflects a passionate interest in her job. It can also be very helpful to ask the individual to talk about what kind of work she is passionate about. If you have a trusting relationship with the employee, she will likely be candid in her answer, enabling you to assess your employee's passion for the current job.

Preferences

Next, you will want to assess whether the person's preferences match up with the task involved for the targeted strength. To do so, think about what preferences a person must have to be comfortable completing a given task, then talk to your employee about whether he possesses that particular set of preferences. In addition, assessments such as those mentioned earlier (the *Work Preferences Inventory* and the *Work Preferences Questionnaire*) can be used to determine an employee's preferences. By examining both passion and preferences, you and the employee will gain insight into whether a lack of fit is constraining performance for the given task.

DOES THE PERSON DISPLAY FIT FOR THE ORGANIZATIONAL CULTURE AND VALUES?

Last, you will want to spend some time with the employee assessing whether she has the right fit for working, not just on the task, but at the organization, given its culture and values. Regardless of how much an employee has the fit to engage in a certain task, if she must complete that task in the context of an organizational culture and set of values she does not appreciate or support, her performance will likely be affected.[4]

For example, an employee might have the passion and preference (fit) for the task of writing press releases generally, but not for writing press releases for an oil company in particular. Although she tries to do a good job of writing press releases and she has been able to fake her passion and preference for working for an oil company during her initial six months, as an environmentalist, she is running out of the energy needed to fake fit and is now finding it difficult to apply her talent to writing press releases for her current company. The employee still writes the releases in a timely manner, but their quality has begun to diminish. This occurs because, although she has the passion and preference to write press releases in general, she does not have the passion and preference to write press releases in the current context of her work at an oil company.

TALENT AND FIT AREN'T EXPANDABLE

If you determine that the talent and fit factor is key to what would normally be called an *expandable* strength, this means that the strength is not so expandable after all—not, at least, to the exemplary level. In other words, you mischaracterized a task as an expandable strength (something with the potential to become exemplary) in step 1 of the process. That's okay. It's not always clear whether someone has the potential to become exemplary at something until you understand the relevant performance factor. Once you make this discovery, you can still work on building this performance—even if not to the exemplary level—or you can set the task aside. Then you can move on to selecting a different expandable strength that *does* have the potential to become exemplary.

Is the Talent and Fit Factor Key for an Exemplary Strength?

The process for determining the key performance factor driving the exemplary strength consists of the following steps:

- Scan the performance factors in the model to see if one factor for the given task stands out to both you and the employee as occurring to a greater degree or in a different form for the employee than for nonexemplary performers.

- If more than one factor is detected, work with the employee to narrow the probable factors to the one factor believed to be most responsible for exemplary performance.

In support of this process, feel free to look at the diagnostic questions used to identify the key factor for the expandable strength, making appropriate modifications. Instead of asking the questions as they stand in the previous section on expandable strengths, however, you can modify them as follows to get at the *difference* between the employee and others who are not performing the given task at the exemplary level.

1. Does the person exhibit physical traits, intellectual ability, and personality characteristics for success at this type of task that are superior to those of nonexemplary employees?

2. Does the person display more passion and preference for working on this type of task than do the other, nonexemplary employees?

3. Does the person display more passion and preference for the organizational culture and values than the other, nonexemplary employees?

An answer of "yes" to any of the above questions may indicate that the talent and fit factor is the key performance factor driving exemplary performance. To repeat, though, these questions are not meant to provide the definitive answer on the issue of the key factor; instead, they are meant to offer helpful data in the larger discussion and assessment that you and the employee will be conducting together to determine the key factor underlying the exemplary strength.

What you are really looking for here is something that seems innate, something within the person that is driving exemplary performance in a specific key responsibility or task. Physical capabilities are the easiest to diagnose. After all, a construction worker who is tall and muscular will have a greater capacity to lift a large amount of weight than one who is short and scrawny. Also, a person's passions and preferences, when responsible for an exemplary strength, will show themselves in many ways, such as through a strong desire to learn all she can about a topic and through the extra effort she makes just because she loves the topic. However, some innate abilities are more difficult to diagnose. Without drilling down into this factor, we won't know if someone just gets it and is "wired" to understand at a deeper level and with greater ease than are most people.

Tools to Compensate for Lack of Talent and Fit

Once you determine that a lack of talent or fit explains the level of performance for an expandable strength, you have options for addressing the issue—or not. Note, however, that the talent and fit tools, unlike the tools offered to address the other factors, are not meant to transform an expandable strength into an exemplary one since it is not possible to achieve an exemplary level of performance without talent and it is not possible to develop greater talent. Instead, these tools are intended to help you compensate for the fact that talent or fit is missing so that the employee can improve performance, even if not to the exemplary level.

JOB RESTRUCTURING

One option is to restructure a person's job profile to exclude tasks related to the so-called expandable strength and then reallocate the task to someone in the department or organization who does have talent and fit for that task. This particular tool represents a rather unorthodox practice because it is typically considered an unaffordable luxury to relieve employees of tasks and responsibilities that they were originally hired to cover. Certainly there are times when relieving an employee of his prescribed tasks is not an option, whether owing to staffing issues or to lack of talented others to handle the given tasks. Yet where reallocation is viable, benefits may arise from learning how to reallocate tasks among team members so that you maximize the team's ability as a whole to achieve exemplary performance. It is also useful that employees who give up a task for which they lack talent or fit will now become available to accept new tasks that do play to their actual talents and fit.

ACCEPTING LESS-THAN-EXEMPLARY PERFORMANCE

Another option would be to do nothing—that is, to simply accept that a person has a ceiling of at-standards or slightly above-standards performance for the given task. If the targeted task occurs in an area of a person's job that is not considered critical, then at-standards or slightly above-standards performance may be a fine level of performance to ultimately accept. Although I do encourage leaders to foster exemplary performance in individuals, note that I am referring to exemplary performance for critical tasks. It is unlikely that individuals will be exemplary at each and every task they perform.

JOB TRANSFER OR TERMINATION

If the lack of talent and fit occurs in a critical area of the employee's job and this lack cannot be addressed by giving the task to another employee, the employee should most likely either be transferred to another job to which she is better suited in terms of talent and fit or be let go from the organization. The first option means finding a new role for the employee within the organization that capitalizes on her strengths. In this way, you may be able to keep a valued employee who has strengths needed in another area of the business. All the organizational knowledge as well as the investment in the individual will remain within the company by using this tool.

It is important to note that my focus in this book is on developing exemplary performance. In the process I've advocated, we focus on strengths. Because the targeted task is considered a strength (even if lacking the potential to be increased to the exemplary level because of the lack of talent or fit), the employee is already performing this task at or slightly above standards. Therefore, it would not make sense to transfer or let the person go just because it is discovered that she cannot reach the exemplary level of performance with this expandable strength. This current tool, transfer or termination, is included to guide those using the model for a separate application: the attempt to raise weaknesses to the performance standards set by the department. In this application, this tool would be a viable option.

I sometimes refer to letting people go as "freeing up their future." Although people laugh at this, it reflects a mind-set of releasing individuals from a situation where they are not performing and allowing them to pursue something that might more closely match their talents. In the short term, this can be difficult for the employee (and for you, the leader). Many thoughts may go through the person's mind, such as "What will I do for money?"; "What will people think of me?"; "Does this mean I'm worthless?"; and "Is there anything I can do well?" However, this change also affords the employee the opportunity to explore her strengths and to help her discover areas of talent and possible roles that would call for those talents. It also affords you, as the leader, the chance to find and develop someone with the right talents for the job from the start.

Leveraging the Exemplary Strength

Because talent is completely individual, it is an impossible task to ask someone to transfer his talent to another individual. But remember, you are not aiming to leverage talent itself but rather the targeted exemplary strength. As a result, you can look for ways that the talented employee can help others become better at the targeted task. To do so, you can turn to many of the tools used to leverage tasks that are driven by the other factors. Specifically, the tools related to knowledge and skills, processes, tools and resources, motivation, clear expectations and accountability, and environment can also be used to leverage talent.

For example, you and the employee can leverage her exemplary strength by identifying the skills and knowledge she uses to complement her talent for the given task and then train, coach, or mentor (skills and knowledge-related tools) others using that information. It's interesting to think about Michael Jordan again here. When the former NBA star decided to engage in an early morning practice routine at his house each day before hitting the required practice, he invited his other teammates to join him. Some did, and although they were not able to absorb Jordan's talents, they were able to benefit from the same training that Jordan used to enrich his talent, and of course gain one more opportunity to observe Jordan in action. Therefore, although Jordan could not transfer his actual talent to others, he was nonetheless able to help raise the play of his teammates by including them in the training he was receiving to sharpen skills and by serving as a role model for his teammates.

Responsibility for Addressing Talent and Fit

Both the leader and the employee play a role in targeting performance related to talent and fit. When it comes to leveraging exemplary strengths, the leader's role is to support the employee in sharing the targeted strength with others (e.g., by authorizing time to train or mentor others), whereas the employee is responsible for making the time to help others become good at the targeted task (e.g., by designing a training class and teaching it). When it comes to addressing the expandable strength, a large part of the responsibility lies with the leader.

As we have seen, talent and fit cannot be increased if they don't exist, so there is little the employee can do to address performance related to talent and fit, beyond informing the leader that talent or fit might be an issue. Instead, as shown by the tools for addressing expandable strengths related to talent and fit, the leader will need to consider getting involved to alter the employee's job profile (delegating certain tasks elsewhere), to transfer the employee into a different position, or to let her go.

Using the Model in the Real World

I once worked with a person (let's call him Mason) at a nonprofit organization. In his job as marketing director, Mason was responsible for graphic design, layout, and editing the copy for the organization's marketing materials. Mason was exemplary at designing graphics and laying out the marketing copy. But he had one area that we felt he should focus on for performance development: his copyediting of the written text. Although Mason usually met organizational standards for copyediting (e.g., he removed all spelling errors, formatted text consistently in bold or italics where needed, and ensured correct text alignment), he was not at the exemplary level of performance. Occasionally, minor errors would appear in final pieces. This shortcoming frustrated Mason, who wanted the materials to be perfect. And it was an important area of performance, because if errors appeared in the marketing materials, potential customers might suspect inconsistent quality of services and be less inclined to work with the organization.

As Mason and I reviewed all of the performance factors, six of the seven factors seemed present and accounted for. For example, Mason had the *skills and knowledge* he needed to copyedit at the exemplary level (he had taken several editing seminars over the years); he had a good understanding of what kind of errors he was trying to avoid because he had a checklist of things to watch out for (*clear expectations*); and he had a consistent *process* for copyediting the materials. The only factor remaining was talent and fit. Mason shared with me that he had always found the copyediting process to be a challenge because he didn't have a natural eye for detail. Whereas text errors seemed to jump out like a sore thumb to other people, Mason had to really concentrate to find them. Years of editing training and practice, a revision to his editing process, and the creation of an editing checklist had not been able to help him raise his performance to exemplary. In other words, addressing the other performance factors had not transformed Mason's performance to the exemplary level. Mason simply lacked natural talent at copyediting.

As a result, we restructured Mason's job profile to exclude copyediting and spun this task off to the two individuals who actually wrote marketing copy. The two writers copyedited each other's work; because they were knowledgeable, skilled, and talented at writing and editing, they were able to raise the quality of copyediting to the exemplary standard. In addition, some of Mason's time was freed up to focus more on the tasks that he did have talent for, such as graphic design and layout. He no longer felt demoralized by a task for which he would never have the potential to be exemplary. As a result, his overall motivation at work increased (a pleasant side effect of applying the right solution).

Conclusion

The talent and fit factor is the most difficult one to diagnose. Many times I have seen a leader label an employee as someone who didn't fit in at the organization or who just would never "get it," only to have a new leader come in and turn around this employee's performance. Talents can be hidden for a variety of reasons, so my best advice to leaders is to be careful about selecting talent and fit as the key factor. If it's not completely obvious to both you and your employee that this is the key factor for the targeted task, then consider focusing on the other factors first. This approach would allow employees to prove to you that they can become exemplary performers by creating action plans around these other factors. The point here is to not jump to the conclusion that the person doesn't have the talent or isn't right for the job. Using the questions to determine whether the talent and fit factor is the reason for the exemplary or expandable strength will help you make the correct diagnosis.

Although talent and fit are discussed first, when it comes to using the Exemplary Performance Model, no factor is more important than another. The most important factor at any given time is the one that applies to the area of performance you are currently targeting. When using the model, you do need to begin somewhere when assessing factors. If you have a hunch about which performance factor is at play, you may want to investigate that particular factor first, then run through the other factors to make sure you're not missing anything. Otherwise, you can arbitrarily decide which factor to begin with and work your way through each of the factors during your review.

Although it can be disappointing to find out that an employee lacks the talent or fit to be exemplary at a given task for his job or for the job as a whole, this discovery can also be enlightening and empowering. Once you know that this factor is what's constraining performance, you will have the insight to develop an effective action plan for addressing the issue. Although talent and fit cannot be taught, learning to recognize that talent and fit are at the heart of a performance issue will nonetheless empower you to make changes in your department to improve overall performance. And although talent and fit are immutable, with some creativity and the right tools, you can deal with this essential performance issue in an effective way.

4

The
Environment
Factor

Anyone who has worked for an erratic manager or survived massive corporate layoffs or tried to stay focused on work tasks when one's personal life is in a stressful period knows the truth of the following statement: environment has a meaningful effect on a person's ability to perform at work.[1] In this chapter I will flesh out the ways that environment can affect a person's performance and will provide guidance on how to determine whether environment is the key factor affecting the targeted performance area (i.e., an exemplary or expandable strength). In addition, I will walk you through the various tools that can be used to address the environment factor in performance, and I will offer insight into how to select the appropriate tool(s) for leveraging or developing the targeted performance area.

> *Environment has a meaningful effect on a person's ability to perform at work.*

The Environment Defined

As noted in chapter 2, environment refers to the physical, emotional, and interpersonal elements that form the context in which a person works (work environment) and lives (personal environment). Although existing performance development models acknowledge the effect of work environment on performance, no model (to my knowledge) yet includes personal environment (or what is more commonly referred to as "personal life") as one of the possible factors for employee performance. Yet anyone who has been employed knows from experience that personal life does have an effect on one's performance at work. If an employee's marriage is ending, his loved one is seriously ill, or he is struggling to meet his financial obligations, there is a good chance that he will bring that stress to work in some form or another. In turn, that stress will likely affect the employee's performance. Even a happy personal event, like the birth of a child, can affect a person's work performance. Although most of us try to leave our personal issues outside the workplace, it is often impossible to do so.

Work Environment

The work environment is made up of the physical, emotional, and interpersonal elements that create the atmosphere in which a person works. The following list represents the components that together make up the work environment at any organization:

- Organizational culture
- Policies and procedures
- Interpersonal relationships
- Workplace design
- Climate created by past and present events

ORGANIZATIONAL CULTURE

Organizational culture covers the customary practices and norms for behavior in a given department or organization or, in simpler terms, the way people typically act and are expected to act in an organization. Organizational culture also includes such things as the group's values, stories and myths about the history of the group, group rituals, and shoptalk (the language commonly used by the group to talk about itself and the department).[2] The structure of an organization (e.g.,

TABLE 4 **Examples of Organizational Culture**

CULTURE SUBCOMPONENT	EXAMPLE
Customary practices	• New employees are put on a three-month provisional status. • Suits are worn to meetings with outside clients. • Employees who share ideas that get implemented at the organization are rewarded.
Behavioral norms	• People stop by the coffee room for a chat before starting the workday. • Employees refrain from making personal phone calls at work. • People come in to work even when sick.
Values	• Change is not desirable. • Downtime from work (vacations, holidays) is important. • Spending time each week developing your performance is essential (my personal favorite!).
Stories and myths	• Miguel (the former VP of HR) got fired for disagreeing with Elizabeth (the CEO). • Lisa was promoted because she is the boss's daughter-in-law. • The company founder used to make personal visits to every employee on Christmas day.
Group rituals	• Employees' birthdays are celebrated with a cake. • People go out to Friday night happy hour.
Shop talk	• People use jargon and acronyms ("How's the PRD coming along for the learning event DCT?").
Organizational structure and interaction attitudes	• In the authoritarian structure, managers are discouraged from socializing outside of work with subordinates. • In the inclusive structure, people of all roles and ranks are encouraged to provide suggestions on how to improve company systems and processes.

hierarchical or flat) and the attitudes within it about how employees of varying positions and ranks (e.g., management or nonmanagement) should interact also contribute to an organization's culture. Table 4 provides examples of each of the components of organizational culture.

To a large extent, the culture of an organization has an impact on performance.[3] To test this impact, you can change the seating of people in the office or institute a perk for employees such as a one-hour lunch. Each of these items has an impact on the culture of the organization (e.g., changing seating might lead to different interpersonal relationships; instituting a one-hour lunch might lead to a more relaxed work environment). This change in organizational culture, in turn, has an impact on how people think of the organization and on whether they want to do a great job (perform at an exemplary level) or just perform at standards. So the culture of the organization, the department, and the team can have an impact on performance in a positive or negative way.

POLICIES AND PROCEDURES

Work environment is also composed of the policies and procedures that dictate the rules of that environment (e.g., dress code, phone usage, personal time off, etc.). In most cases, policies and procedures are written and are communicated through on-the-job training or a company manual. The way in which a company informs employees of policies and procedures as well as the number of policies and procedures in place contribute to the work environment. For example, many companies have a policy manual that dictates standards for behaviors, procedures, and benefits. This manual helps people understand things such as when they can start receiving benefits, how much vacation time they have, how to file a grievance, what the consequences of excessive absenteeism are, and whether they will be paid while serving on a jury. These become the guiding "rules" for the company.

INTERPERSONAL RELATIONSHIPS

The people in one's workplace and the quality of relationships that one has with these people also contribute to work environment. Figure 6 displays the different interpersonal relationships at work.

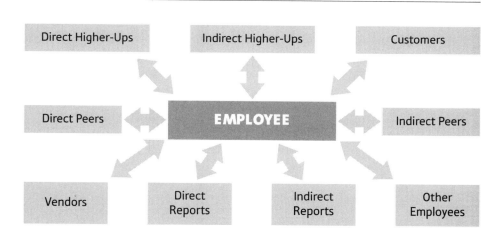

FIGURE 6   **Interpersonal Relationships
That Contribute to the Work Environment**

One is surrounded by people at work: peers and colleagues, managers, senior leaders, direct reports, indirect reports, and possibly customers and vendors. How one gets along with these individuals contributes to one's sense of the work environment—whether it's friendly or hostile, nurturing or punishing, or encouraging or discouraging, for example. The power of interpersonal relationships at work to influence performance is shown in the result of a Gallup study that revealed that those who feel they have a best friend at work (among other things) show superior performance.[4] (The results of this study led to the creation of the popular Gallup Q-12 survey, which assesses employee engagement; see Gallup.com for various studies and information.)

WORKPLACE DESIGN

The workplace design component of work environment refers to the physical layout of the place a person works, such as how desks are placed in relation to one another (close together, far apart), how work spaces are separated (office walls, high cubicle walls, low cubicle walls), how equipment is set up at a given workstation (haphazardly, ergonomically), the degree of general tidiness throughout the office (neat, messy), and so forth. Workplace design can also refer to those conditions that create the sensory aspect of the work environment—things such as noise level, light level, and room temperature. A large body of research on human factors engineering (i.e., ergonomics) has linked workplace design to performance. (Identifying the *absence* of items such as desks, computers, and cubicle walls—rather than that they are designed a certain way—points to a tool and resource issue rather than to a work environment issue.)[5]

Let me make this issue more concrete with a personal story.

The wall of the hallway of an office where I previously worked was lined with file cabinets. When our administrative assistant had files open, the hall was impassable. This forced me to go a different direction—up one flight of stairs, down another hall-way, and down one flight of stairs—to get to the conference room I needed. It was actually much easier to detour than to ask our administrative assistant to pick up her files and move her chair for three seconds while I walked by. Although no one, in-cluding me, minded this situation and everyone grew accus-tomed to it, it was very inefficient. Wasting a few extra minutes once or twice walking down the alternate path I took to the con-ference room was no big deal. However, if one counted up all the minutes I spent repeating this pattern a few times a week, the number was substantial. If the hallway had been redesigned to become passable at all times, I would have had more time to spend each week executing tasks and key responsibilities, which in turn might have raised the level of my performance outcomes. A large body of research on the value of ergonomic workplace design underscores the benefit of such design on performance at work.

CLIMATE IN THE WORKPLACE

Climate in the workplace refers to the feeling, conditions, or mood that has been created at the workplace as a result of current or past events. Significant events that tend to affect the work climate include occur-rences such as the departure of an employee, mergers and acquisitions, layoffs, job restructuring, and rapid company growth. Events such as these can lead to work environments that are unstable, hostile, or chaotic. For example, when an organization experiences a reduction in force, the remaining employees often feel overwhelmed by the increased workload, scared that they will be next to lose their jobs, and upset owing to the loss of people they used to enjoy working with. In some cases, the same kinds of events can lead to work environments that are more enjoyable, more stable, more supported, or more friendly. For example, as an organization expands its operations, this frequently creates opportunities for advancement. Or when a difficult employee leaves, the individuals as well as the team typically perform at a much higher level after the departure. It is amazing how one "bad apple" can have an impact on an entire team.

The past-and-present-events component of work environment also hinges on events taking place outside a company—whether in the industry as a whole, in the business world in general, in the country at large, or in the global community. Significant events in this category include such things as innovations in the industry, legislative action that affects how a company conducts business, social movements (e.g., going green to have a lighter impact on the natural environment), and economic shifts in the country for the better or worse. Organizational responses to external events (e.g., increased bonuses, closure of factories, purchase of an additional facility) contribute to the kind of work environment employees face every day. People may be distracted, concerned, or motivated, depending on the outside events and the way that an organization responds to these events.

Personal Environment

Personal environment refers to the physical, emotional, and interpersonal elements that make up the atmosphere in which a person lives. Although keeping the personal environment and the work environment separate has been a long-standing American ideal, in reality, doing so is a challenge if not an impossibility. Additionally, some feel that this sharp separation is outdated.[6] For example, when children get sick, employed parents have to leave work early to make doctor visits. When a home health aide calls an employee at work to inform her of her mother's fall down the stairs, the employee has to take the call. And when an employee is experiencing extreme emotions due to personal life issues (such as a death in the family, a new baby, a marital

TABLE 5 **Components of the Personal Environment**

COMPONENT	DESCRIPTION	EXAMPLE
Personal health and mental well-being	The current state of one's physical and mental health	Diagnosis of cancer, panic attacks, sleep deprivation from frequent travel
Family life	One's family relationships and the events occurring within the family domain	Birth of a child, death of a family member, sick children, aging parents, marital problems
Social network	One's friends, acquaintances, and group affiliations and the events occurring within one's social network	Political in-fighting at church, sickness of a friend, conflict provoked by neighbors
Financial life	One's degree of financial stability and the events occurring within the domain of someone's personal finances	Mortgage default, loss of job by spouse, inheritance
Personal events	Things that happen to the employee outside the workplace	Car accident, house flood, identity theft, towed car

breakup, or a new romantic relationship), those emotions will likely affect the way a person engages at work. A study by Rabi S. Bhagat confirms that stressful life events do have a detrimental effect on employee performance.[7] When trying to understand the root cause of performance, one thus needs to consider the role of personal environment. Components of the personal environment are presented in table 5.

Although an employee's personal environment is created by all of the things going on in his or her life outside of the workplace, the effects of these outside events and experiences will follow the employee into the workplace. If the employee's personal environment is calm and stable, she may carry this calmness into the workplace, where she is able to focus and be productive. If the employee's personal environment is stressful or chaotic, she is likely to have difficulty concentrating, spend work time on personal calls, or talk with colleagues more than usual. A study of those who are suffering from sleep deprivation (an area within the personal health category of personal environment) owing to frequent business travel revealed its negative effect on work performance.[8] How one is faring in his or her personal life—the state of one's personal environment—has the potential to be a key driver of performance at work.

Is the Environment Factor the Key to an Expandable Strength?

When trying to identify whether the environment is the key factor at play for an expandable strength, you will want to ask your employee the following three questions:

1. Are there internal issues going on in the work group or the organization, or outside events that are having a negative impact on the work group or organization, that are ultimately constraining the employee's ability to perform at the exemplary level?

2. Does the employee's physical work setting affect performance in a way that makes exemplary performance difficult?

3. Could something happening outside work be having an impact on the employee's ability to perform at the exemplary level?

1. ARE THERE INTERNAL OR EXTERNAL ISSUES THAT CONSTRAIN PERFORMANCE?

If an employee answers yes to this question, you will want to investigate further to determine the nature of the employee's concern or complaint. The answer to this follow-up question will likely point to one of the components of work environment discussed earlier in the chapter—organizational culture, policies and procedures, interpersonal relationships, workplace design, or climate created by past or present events—and will provide you with insight into the appropriate tools to use to leverage or develop performance.

2. DOES THE PHYSICAL WORK SETTING HAVE AN IMPACT ON PERFORMANCE?

Employees may be reticent about issues with their physical work environment, either because they assume nothing can be done to address them or because they are embarrassed to admit their discomfort. For example, someone who needs quiet to concentrate might not mention that the noise level of the work environment is distracting because she figures there is no alternative to the present situation, or because she considers it a weakness that she needs quiet and is reluctant to share this "weakness." Of course, some employees may feel entirely comfortable letting you know about their issues with their physical work environment. It depends on the given employee and the quality of communication between the two of you. In any case, if you've observed or been informed that the physical environment may be an issue for the employee, or if you are having trouble identifying the key performance factor, be sure to probe about this aspect of environment to see whether anything may be constraining performance of the targeted task.

3. COULD SOMETHING HAPPENING OUTSIDE OF WORK BE AFFECTING PERFORMANCE?

If a person answers yes to this question, investigate further, in a sensitive and diplomatic way. Naturally, this is delicate territory, as you don't want to push the employee to share more than she is comfortable discussing. The goal is not to encourage the employee to share the depth of her current personal issues or even specifics but to gain enough insight into the issue so that you and the employee will be able to explore how it might be affecting performance (and, ultimately, develop a useful action plan to address this issue).

Is the Environment the Key Enabler for an Exemplary Strength?

As I indicated in the previous chapter, the process for determining the key performance factor driving the exemplary strength consists of the following steps:

- Scan the performance factors in the model to see if one factor for the given task stands out to both you and the employee as occurring to a greater degree or in a different form for the employee than for nonexemplary performers.

- If more than one factor is detected, work with the employee to narrow the probable factors to the one factor believed to be most responsible for exemplary performance.

In support of this process, feel free to look at the diagnostic questions used to identify the key factor for the expandable strength, making appropriate modifications. Instead of asking the questions in the previous section on expandable strengths, questions that assess whether work environment is having a *negative* impact on employee performance, you can modify these questions to get at whether work environment is having a *positive* impact on employee performance.

1. Are there internal events going on in the work group or the organization or outside events that are having a positive impact on the work group or organization that are affecting the employee's performance?

2. Does the employee's physical work setting have an impact on performance in a positive way?

3. Could something happening in the employee's personal life be having a positive impact on the employee's performance?

An answer of yes to one or more of the previous questions could indicate that the environment is the key driver of exemplary performance for the targeted strength. When my wife and I had our first child, having this (wonderful) new responsibility made me realize how important it was for me to excel at work in order to be seen as a top performer, to avoid being cut in case there was a corporate restructuring, and possibly to be eligible for a pay increase at the time of an annual review. In this case, my life experience of having a child may have been the cause of one or more exemplary strengths. To assess whether environment is the key performance factor for an exemplary strength, you can ask the three diagnostic questions and then work with the employee to run through the other factors to see whether environment appears to be the factor most contributing to the exemplary strength.

Tools to Develop or Leverage Performance Related to the Environment

There are many tools to use to develop an expandable strength or to leverage an exemplary strength when the environment is determined to be the factor most responsible for the strength.

DEVELOPING THE EXPANDABLE STRENGTH

Given that the environment factor has so many components to it—organizational culture, policies and procedures, interpersonal relationships, workplace design, climate created by past and present events, personal health and well-being, family life, social network, financial life, and personal events—there is a wide range of tools that can be used to develop strengths that are constrained by the environment factor.

Organizational Culture Survey

An organizational culture survey is designed to assess the factors that contribute to the organizational culture and the effectiveness of each factor. This type of survey is typically conducted when you are examining the organization or a department or function rather than an individual. Therefore, when focusing on an individual, you would most likely not use this particular tool. I include it here because, as I will review later, the model can be used beyond the limits I observe in this book, to address performance at the macro level as well as at the individual level. (See chapter 11 for a more complete explanation.)

Employee Assistance Program (EAP)

EAPs are programs that provide counseling or assistance (e.g., counseling, identification of day care options) to individuals, typically at no expense, by a licensed professional. They have become increasingly common at organizations and can serve as a wonderful tool to help employees address personal environment issues that are constraining performance from reaching the exemplary level. For example, an employee who has lost a family member recently might be able to use the EAP to obtain grief counseling, and an employee who is fighting for child custody might be able to obtain legal assistance. In both cases, the resources of the EAP might help employees reduce stress in their personal lives and improve their work performance in the process.

For most leaders, discovering that an employee has an issue that may be helped by participation in an EAP can be challenging. Although leaders are not counselors and cannot provide advice, they can still build awareness of the EAP benefit and encourage employees to take the initiative to include use of the EAP in their action plans (step 3). When referring an employee to an EAP, keep in mind that this information must be kept confidential and should not be repeated to anyone except your human resources professional.

Assessment and Redesign of Physical Workplace

This tool involves taking a formal or an informal assessment of the physical workplace (i.e., the ergonomics) in an effort to pinpoint the exact areas and conditions that are affecting performance. This tool involves altering or redesigning identified areas and conditions to raise the level of employee performance and can serve as an action item in step 3, where you develop a plan. For example, if the assessment revealed that your employee's energy level decreases without natural light, you might arrange to supply the employee with a full-spectrum lamp, which simulates natural light. Or, for example, if an employee needs a quiet work environment (work conditions) to perform at her maximal level, you might relocate her to another part of the office or give her a different work shift (evening rather than daytime).

Reassignment or Transfer

If the environment of the current job cannot be altered or redesigned to address the performance constraint, reassignment or transfer (i.e., moving an employee to a new job in the department or organization) might be considered. This tool is useful for those instances in which an employee doesn't get along with the supervisor (i.e., leader). While coworkers might be able to work with the supervisor without any problems, for some reason this relationship is getting in the way of the given employee's performance. Of course, when this situation occurs, it is difficult to diagnose because most people are not going to tell their boss that he or she is the problem. However, if you find yourself in this situation, you will most likely have an idea that you and the employee don't get along; if so, the conflictual relationship is interfering with your employee's performance. If this is the case and the situation permits, you might choose to transfer the person to work for a different leader.

Policy Manual

A policy manual details workplace behaviors, benefits, and procedures. In some cases, work environment issues can be addressed when a leader initiates the creation, revision, or removal of policies to diminish aspects of the environment believed to lead to the gap between expandable and exemplary performance. For example, the institution of a policy specifically addressing what a hostile work environment is and the consequences of creating one can sometimes deter people who would otherwise act in a way that might create an uncomfortable environment for other employees.

Benefits

In some cases, adjusting existing employee benefits (e.g., time off and health, vision, dental, life, and disability insurance) or providing new benefits will remove environmental barriers to performance. For example, providing disability insurance may remove a concern a person has about what happens if she gets hurt outside of work. This recurring concern may have been distracting the person and not allowing her to focus on her performance of the targeted task.

The benefits a company offers also communicate a message to employees. For example, if an organization is lagging in terms of the benefits it offers, employees may think the company doesn't care about them. This, in turn, has an impact on employees' intent to stay with the organization. In fact, according to a 2004 study by the Corporate Leadership Council of 50,000 employees at fifty-nine global companies, increasing satisfaction with total compensation (pay plus benefits) provides up to a 21 percent increase in employees' intent to stay. Yet, also of note, this increasing satisfaction yields only a 9 percent increase in effort, indicating that benefits, while an important factor in retention, can drive performance only so far.[9] Thus, when using benefits as a tool to address the factor for an expandable strength, keep in mind that although this will remove a road block, which may help improve performance to some degree, you may still subsequently need to select other tools to drive performance to the exemplary level.

Personal Finances and Planning

This tool involves connecting employees to financial assistance, usually in the form of financial counseling, to help them plan the use of their personal funds and plan for future life events. Like EAPs, this tool may eliminate or reduce stress in an employee's life, and in turn increase performance. For example, providing an employee stressed about making house payments with financial advice that enables him to balance his budget might also enhance his ability to concentrate at work, which might in turn improve the targeted expandable strength.

Communication

This tool involves the exchange of information between two parties and is extremely useful during times of organizational or external change. In particular, the leader provides as much detailed information as possible to the employee to relieve employee concerns about organizational or external change and to help the employee focus on her job (including, of course, the targeted task). For example, if your organization has made an announcement that it plans to purchase a competitor, you may institute a weekly update in which you communicate as much information as you can on what impact this will have on the company, the department, and the team. This weekly update will help maintain a stable work environment for your employees and reduce potential stresses that might constrain performance.

Social and Professional Network

This tool involves tapping into one's social network as well as one's professional network (the people outside and within the organization whom the person can contact) for information, support, leads, ideas, and so forth. With this tool, the leader encourages the employee to tap into existing or new networks for support that will help the employee resolve or deal with the environmental issues that constrain the expandable strength. For example, you may have your employee ask a well-respected colleague whom he knows from a professional association about how she handled developing a particular expandable strength when she was in a similar situation. Her input might provide your employee with a different perspective and new ideas on how to develop an expandable strength.

TABLE 6 **Tools for Addressing the Environment Factor**

TOOL	HOW TO USE FOR LEVERAGING	EXAMPLE
Employee assistance program (EAP)	The leader communicates the availability of this program if an employee brings up an appropriate issue.	An employee who has used the EAP to address an issue and refocus on work can communicate the EAP's value to a co-worker.
Assessment and redesign of physical workplace	The leader makes arrangements to implement ergonomics used by the exemplary employee for other employees.	Monitor stands are provided to employees to elevate the computer screen to eye level to eliminate a sore neck.
Reassignment or transfer	The leader moves the employee into a new role so that the employee can have a positive effect on the environment and thus on the performance of other employees.	An employee who was transferred to work in the same role for another team discusses the importance of workplace relationships with her team.
Policy manual	The leader initiates the creation or revision of policies to foster the environment believed to contribute to the employee's exemplary strength so others' performance can improve.	The policy on making suggestions is revised to make it faster and more effective.

LEVERAGING THE EXEMPLARY STRENGTH

Many of the tools that can be used for developing an expandable strength related to the environment factor can also be used to leverage an exemplary strength related to the environment factor. Table 6 provides an overview of how these tools can be used to leverage a strength, along with examples.

When the environment is determined to be the factor for an exemplary strength, these tools can be used in a variety of ways. Although

TABLE 6 CONT'D

TOOL	HOW TO USE FOR LEVERAGING	EXAMPLE
Benefits (e.g., time off and health, vision, dental, life, and disability insurance)	The leader institutes or changes a specific benefit to address concerns employees may have.	Benefits are expanded to include an additional personal day for taking time off for annual checkups.
Personal finances and planning	Help is provided for the creation or revision of a personal budget or investments.	Employee discusses how the company 401k plan helped her plan for retirement and ease her mind about her future.
Communication	Information is provided about an organizational change.	Employee with an exemplary strength in communicating change is made responsible for gathering feedback from employees to inform her leader of their opinions.
Social and professional network	Employee connects others in the organization to his or her network of contacts, where appropriate.	Employee helps a co-worker by putting him in touch with an expert from her professional association.

only a few examples were presented here, there are many more options. Try to be inventive and think outside the box to get the most out of these tools.

Responsibility for Addressing the Environment

Sometimes, your employees will play a role in addressing performance strengths related to the environment factor. For example, if an employee is struggling with a personal life issue, he or she has the right to access available services like the EAP or financial planning to alleviate stress from personal environment concerns. Employees are also in a wonderful position to bring to your attention any work environment issues they are facing so as to enlist your support as the leader. Oftentimes with the environment factor, though, you as the leader will be the one (rather than the employee himself or herself) responsible for resolving environmental concerns that are affecting the employee's performance since you, far more than your employee, will have the power needed to implement the tools for addressing the environment. For example, as a leader, you can oversee, or at least initiate, a job transfer, changes to the organizational policy manual, or benefits adjustments.

There may, of course, be limits to your power, too, and in such cases, you might discover that responsibility for the environmental concerns raised by your employee do not lie entirely within your domain. Instead, they might lie in part, if not completely, within a different department, with more senior leaders, or with an actor outside the organization (as in the case of legislation by Congress). If this situation should arise, your goals should be:

- Do what you can within your control

- "Bubble" the rest of the issue up the management chain or across to the right department

- Devise a plan to work around the challenge in the environment

DOING WHAT YOU CAN WITHIN YOUR CONTROL

Although as a leader you may not always have control over the larger organizational strategies that will be affecting your department (and contributing to the work environment), there are often things you can do to foster a positive environment. For example, imagine that you are going through the development model with an employee and that when you try to understand the cause of the targeted expandable strength, she says that her environment is the reason she is not performing better. When you probe further, she says that the real issue is that the organization seems to be changing, and she is not sure whether her role will continue to be needed. In this case, you may not be able to change the restructuring plans of senior management, but there are still actions you can take. You may create a plan to communicate information about organizational plans on a weekly basis to her and the team. You may be able to talk with your leader to get a clearer idea of whether there will be an impact on your team and, if so, what it will be. You may also be able to work with the employee to document and communicate the value of her work. These types of things will most likely ease your employee's fears, as well as those of her teammates.

"BUBBLING UP" THE MANAGEMENT
CHAIN OR ACROSS THE ORGANIZATION

After you have made an action plan to do what you can within your control, you will want to follow up by communicating the environmental issues to the appropriate people, those who *can* make changes in your organization. In some cases, this person will be your own manager; in others, you may need to have a conversation with someone in a different department (e.g., information technology). Your role is to take responsibility for transferring the valuable, credible information you have gained from your employee (reports of low morale, reports of broken processes, etc.) up the chain of command or to the relevant area of the organization.

DEVISING A PLAN TO WORK AROUND
THE CHALLENGE IN THE ENVIRONMENT

At times, it might seem as though there is truly nothing within your control that you can do to address an environmental challenge. Also, you may find that you have communicated the environmental challenge to your leader and nothing is getting done. Yet you might be able to work around the environmental challenge by finding a way to address it in a creative or nontraditional manner.

For example, I once had an employee who had a cubicle near the entrance to the department. Anyone entering or leaving the department walked by her cubicle. This proved to be distracting to her. Unfortunately, we couldn't move her to another cubicle because they were all taken and no one wanted to move. In communicating this challenge to my boss, I found out that we couldn't get any budget to create new walls, so she had to make do with the cubicle she had.

To work around this situation, the employee brought in a clean sheet, hung it from the ceiling to make a full wall between her cubicle and the walkway, and decorated it by pinning on motivational sayings that people in the hall could read. She also politely asked people to respect the team by avoiding loud noises. Within one week, the noise level by her office had dropped to the point that her work quality and quantity began to increase. Although the employee was not able to resolve the environmental challenge in a traditional way (e.g., by relocating her work space), with some creativity and ingenuity she was able to adjust her environment and improve her performance.

Using the Model in the Real World

I once worked as the trainer for the reservations department of a company that sold vacation packages. In this role, I was responsible for people during the first three weeks they were employed at the company. Gary was in the third class I taught there. He appeared to be very professional and seemed to like the work. After the second week of class, I sat down with him to have a discussion about his performance while in training. One strength we brought to the surface was that he was good at customer service and that in his role plays, his partners commented that he had a great ability to listen to concerns. Unfortunately, these good customer service skills were compromised in his real work setting when there was noise around, because noise distracted Gary and made him feel uncomfortable.

In probing deeper, we discovered that Gary became uncomfortable because it was hard for him to focus on the customer when there was noise around him. Targeting listening as the expandable strength, we started to determine the key performance factor by asking the questions associated with each factor (see appendix B). We covered the talent and fit factor first. Gary loved helping customers, displayed the cognitive ability and traits needed for this type of work, and supported the values of the organization. However, each time he had been successful working with customers (in past jobs), he had had his own office and was able to close the door to block out other noise. When we investigated further, we found that in the call center at our company, people worked in cubicles with low walls. At times, the atmosphere became noisy (though never so noisy that customers complained). The noise level made it difficult for Gary to listen and interact with customers in an exemplary way. In other words, Gary was able to perform better in a quiet *environment* than in a noise-filled environment, and the environment factor seemed to be most responsible for the gap between expandable and exemplary listening skills.

As a result, we decided to redesign Gary's workplace conditions to be less noisy. We were able to put Gary in a less noisy work setting by transferring him to the late shift—one in which there were fewer employees around him and consequently there was less noise. It just so happened that we were having difficulty recruiting people for this team, so the change worked to the advantage of the department as well as of Gary. By altering Gary's work conditions from noisy to quiet, we were able to help Gary improve the task of listening to customers to the exemplary level.

Conclusion

Environment is a straightforward concept—the physical, emotional, and interpersonal elements that make up the atmosphere in which a person works and lives. Yet with so many elements making up the environment factor—organizational culture, policies and procedures, interpersonal relationships, workplace design, climate created by past and present events, personal health and well-being, family life, social network, financial life, and personal events—it could be easy to overlook an area that might be affecting performance. By using the diagnostic questions provided in this chapter, you and your employee can stay on track. Although these questions are general, they are typically quite effective at encouraging employees to raise issues related to any of the elements involved with the environment factor. You can also review the components of the work environment presented in in this chapter (summarized in a bulleted list), along with the components of the personal environment (summarized in table 5).

5

The Tools and Resources Factor

Have you ever found yourself in a situation in which you were trying to do your job, but you didn't have all of the supplies you needed to get the job done? Or perhaps the equipment you were using to complete a job was slow, problematic, or unreliable? If so, you've had direct experience of how tools and resources—or lack thereof—can affect your performance.

For example, let's say your computer is five years old and barely meets the minimum requirements for the new inventory software rolled out at your company. The computer is capable of operating the software, but it runs slowly, so it takes you three times longer than it takes your colleagues to order new inventory for their respective departments. The slowness of your computer takes time away from other essential functions of your job and keeps you from reaching exemplary performance in multiple areas.

If you have ample resources to do your job, you may find that the tools and resources factor is the one that allows you to attain exemplary performance, while your competitors in the industry fall behind.

This is just one example of how the tools and resources factor—the focus of this chapter—can negatively affect performance. In other cases, the tools and resources factor can drive exemplary performance. For example, if you have ample resources to do your job (e.g., a large staff, liberal funding), you may find that the tools and resources factor is the one that allows you to attain exemplary performance, while your competitors in the industry fall behind.

The tools and resources factor is one of the most straightforward to identify because many tools and resources are concrete, making them easier for you and an employee to recognize, describe, and analyze than factors such as talent and fit or motivation, which represent abstract concepts. In this chapter I will run through the list of common tools and resources that play a role in driving performance and will offer guidance on what questions to ask when identifying whether this factor is the primary issue for a targeted strength. I will also discuss tools for leveraging or developing a performance area driven by a tools and resources factor.

Tools and Resources Defined

The tools and resources factor refers to the physical items (tools) and useful supply sources (resources) that an employee needs to do his or her job. If your employee does not have the concrete items (e.g., computer, fast printer, company car) or supply sources (e.g., time, money, info) necessary to complete a task or to complete a task well, then the tools and resources factor is at play in this performance area. Here are some examples of tools and resources issues and how they have an impact on performance:

- Tamara doesn't have a phone that handles conference calls, so she has to make conference calls in the meeting room, where she does not have access to her computerized customer database. Thus, she isn't able to access valuable customer information while on conference calls, making it difficult for her to generate price quotes on the spot, which frustrates her customers.

- Jean-Paul doesn't have a private office that can accommodate client visits, so he meets clients at a local coffee shop, where it can be hard to find a seat and the noise level is high. As a result, he feels flustered at client meetings because he often has to conduct them while standing up and talking over loud noise. His ability to win clients over is diminished.

- Elizabeth doesn't have a laminating machine at her company, so she has to walk down the street to the copy store every time she needs to make an ID for a new employee. She is therefore far less efficient at this job task than she could be, delaying her completion of other job tasks.

Clearly, a lack of tools and resources has an effect on performance. I will share examples of the positive ways in which tools and resources can drive performance a little later in the chapter. First, let's examine the different kinds of tools and resources.

Tools

Tools are defined as the items that employees need to do their jobs. They are the tangible items that employees use and, often, take for granted until they aren't there. For example, we don't think about how grateful we are for our phone or ergonomic keyboard unless they break. Without these concrete tools, we probably would not be able to do our jobs.

Tools include the following:

- Equipment (e.g., computer, phone, fax machine, copier)
- Technology (e.g., software programs, security system, GPS system)
- Job aids (e.g., lists, flow charts, prompts)
- Materials (e.g., paper, pens, packing supplies; circuits for people who build circuit boards)

The examples above apply mainly to a traditional corporate setting, but plenty of examples could be drawn from heavy industry as well, such as forklifts (equipment), computer software to run the assembly line (technology), new-hire checklist for operating a concrete pump (job aids); and cement (materials). As you reflect on your particular organization and industry, many other examples of tools will likely come to mind.

Resources

Resources are the supply sources we leverage in order to get our jobs done. They are sometimes tangible and sometimes intangible. Resources include:

- Financial resources
- Time
- Information and data
- Access to people

FINANCIAL RESOURCES

The term *financial resources* refers to the money directly or indirectly needed to perform a task or fulfill a key responsibility. If financial resources are lacking, a person might, for example:

- Not have enough money to hire the people necessary to get a job done in the desired time
- Not have the money to buy top-of-the-line supplies, and the quality of products manufactured by the organization suffers
- Not have the budget to hire an individual with the skill level needed for a specific job
- Not have the budget to purchase the quantity of materials needed to meet customer needs (e.g., not enough portable cribs for hotel guests) or production levels

These points represent examples of financial resources affecting performance in a negative way. Financial resources can also, of course, positively affect performance, as in the case of an organization's securing a budget to hire top talent for a specific job that is critical to success, or its receiving a grant to cover the cost of top-of-the-line health care equipment.

TIME

Time is one of the most important resources that employees have, given that time is necessary to complete every single task an employee is charged with (from taking client calls to writing up reports to researching the competition to developing performance). Unlike many resources, time is finite and cannot be created. What can be done to address the resource of time is to help employees *free up* previously occupied time by removing nonessential tasks or speeding up current tasks so that they can devote more time to important work that has an impact. For example, you can authorize an employee to delegate certain tasks to a subordinate, or you can purchase updated equipment to help the employee complete a certain task more quickly; in both cases, these changes will free up some time in the employee's schedule.

INFORMATION

There are two aspects to the resource of information. The first aspect is whether employees have the facts they need to do their jobs. The facts may include being informed of a meeting, policy change, or price change. The second aspect of the information or data resource is having *accurate* information. For example, employees may receive a meeting notice, but if this notice states the wrong time (inaccurate information), people's performance will be affected.

ACCESS TO PEOPLE

This resource refers to people's ability to interact with the individuals whom they need to talk with in order to do their jobs. Sometimes, organizations put up barriers and don't allow people to communicate with other people directly. As a result, an employee might have to

1. go through his or her boss,

2. who goes to the other person's boss,

3. who asks the person the necessary question and then,

4. reports the answer to the original employee's boss,

5. who then finally tells the employee.

This kind of indirect access and communication can lead to an inefficient process (five steps instead of one!) and can diminish performance. By contrast, if someone is given access to the right people, she can quickly get the accurate information needed to do her job well.

Table 7 contains examples of how each of the previously described tools and resources might affect performance.

TABLE 7 **Examples of Tools and Resources Issues**

TOOL OR RESOURCE	EXAMPLE	POTENTIAL KEY FACTOR FOR . . .
Equipment	Since I work in the field a lot, I need a cell phone so that I can keep in contact with my customers. Since I don't have a cell phone, I miss a lot of sales opportunities.	Expandable strength
Technology	I use the advanced features of Microsoft Excel to create a pivot table, which allows me to communicate budget information in an exemplary way.	Exemplary strength
Job aids	If I had a list of the vacation packages we offer on one sheet, I wouldn't have to spend time looking up that information and frustrating the customer with long wait times.	Expandable strength
Materials	I keep five pens in my apron so that my customers can sign their checks immediately and not have to wait for me to go get a pen.	Exemplary strength

Is the Tools and Resources Factor Key to an Expandable Strength?

The following three questions will help you determine whether the tools and resources factor is the key factor preventing the expandable strength from becoming exemplary.

1. Does the employee have the tools needed to execute the task at the exemplary level?

2. Does the employee have the resources needed to execute the task at the exemplary level?

3. If the employee were given additional tools or resources, would exemplary performance be more likely?

TABLE 7 CONT'D

TOOL OR RESOURCE	EXAMPLE	POTENTIAL KEY FACTOR FOR . . .
Financial resources	Unlike other supervisors, I was able to purchase the hard hats for my crew so that we didn't receive an OSHA violation or experience a preventable work-related injury.	Exemplary strength
Time	I am so busy writing reports that never get read that I don't have time to follow up with my manager on the status of important projects.	Expandable strength
Information	I didn't know our equipment prices had changed and have been selling a high quantity of goods, but at last year's prices.	Expandable strength
Access to people	If I could talk directly with Mohammed, we could sort this out in a few minutes.	Expandable strength

DOES THE EMPLOYEE HAVE THE TOOLS AND RESOURCES NEEDED TO EXECUTE THE TASK?

An answer of no to either of the first two diagnostic questions points to tools and resources as a possible key factor constraining the targeted task. Although the answers to these questions are either yes or no, you won't be able to answer them until you first ask, "What are the tools and resources that the employee needs to be exemplary?" So your goals are, first, to determine what tools and resources are necessary for exemplary performance and then to attempt to answer diagnostic questions 1 and 2.

WITH ADDITIONAL TOOLS OR RESOURCES, WOULD EXEMPLARY PERFORMANCE BE MORE LIKELY?

Another way to ask questions 1 and 2—that is, another way to help you and the employee brainstorm on the tools and resources issue—is to ask question 3. Again, this question is really preceded by an open question: "What additional tools or resources would help the employee perform at the exemplary level?" Once this question is answered, the yes or no answer to question 3 will be clear.

The primary goal of the three diagnostic questions is to determine the tools and resources needed for exemplary performance and to compare them to the ones the employee uses. In some cases, it might be clear that the employee lacks the tools or resources to be exemplary; at other times, you or the employee might need to do some research to uncover what tools and resources are used by exemplary performers for the given task.

Is the Tools and Resources Factor Key to an Exemplary Strength?

As indicated in previous chapters, the process for determining the key performance factor driving the exemplary strength consists of the following steps:

- Scan the performance factors in the model to see if one factor for the given task stands out to both you and the employee as occurring to a greater degree or in a different form for the employee than for nonexemplary performers.
- If more than one factor is detected, work with the employee to narrow the probable factors to the one factor believed to be most responsible for exemplary performance.

In support of this process, you can ask a modified version of diagnostic questions 1 and 2 for this factor.

1. Does the employee have tools that are superior to those used by nonexemplary performers for the given task?

2. Does the employee have resources that are superior to those used by nonexemplary performers for the given task?

These questions have been modified to help you assess whether the employee has developed, secured, or found tools or resources that no one else is using and whether these tools enable the employee to perform better than others. Thus, in answering modified questions 1 or 2, your efforts will have two parts. First, you will want to determine whether the tools or resources used by the employee are *different* from those used by others for the targeted task. Second, you will aim to uncover whether these different tools allow the employee to perform *better* than other employees. If the answer to modified questions 1 or 2 is yes, then it's possible that the key factor driving exemplary performance is the tools and resources factor. You can then review the remaining performance factors and work to assess whether tools and resources seems to be the factor *most* responsible for driving exemplary performance.

Tools of the Tools and Resources Factor

Like the factor itself, the tools for addressing a tools and resources issue are quite straightforward and are often concrete. In fact, they map directly to the tools and resources themselves. For example, for an exemplary strength, if your employee has access to special *equipment* that your other employees lack, you can leverage this strength by purchasing similar *equipment* for your other employees. For an expandable strength, if your employee lacks *technology*, for example, the customized financial software necessary to efficiently create budget forecasts, your goal will be to obtain the necessary *technology* for your employee. Ultimately, once you identify which tool or resource is driving performance, you will work with the employee to acquire that tool or resource (for an expandable strength) or you will work as the leader to bring that tool or resource to the rest of the department (for an exemplary strength).

DEVELOPING THE EXPANDABLE STRENGTH

The tools for developing an expandable strength that is constrained primarily by the tools and resources factor are as follows:

- Equipment
- Technology
- Job aids
- Materials
- Financial resources
- Time
- Information
- Access to people

If you discover that the employee needs one of the above items to develop an expandable strength, then the preferable tool is the one that corresponds to the exact tool or resource that is lacking (e.g., provide equipment when equipment is missing; provide financial resources when monies are needed; increase access to people when access to people is lacking). Because the tools to address a tools and resources issue and the issue itself align exactly with each other (equipment to equipment, materials to materials, information to information), the decision about which tool is most appropriate to incorporate into the action plan for the tools and resources factor can be easy.

DEVELOPING WITHOUT THE DESIRED TOOL OR RESOURCE

Although the ideal way to address a tools and resources issue is to provide the exact tool or resource expected to drive performance in the targeted area, there may be times when you won't be able to provide that exact tool or resource because of a lack of funding, company policy, or other organizational constraints. In such cases, you will want to work with the employee to come up with a creative way to deal with the tools and resources issue. A creative way to work around constraints might be any one of the following:

- A solution that gives the person temporary access to the necessary tool or resource if permanent access cannot be secured
- A solution that addresses the performance issue itself without providing the identified missing tool
- A solution that provides an alternate tool or resource if the exact tool or resource can not be secured

In practice, people employ creative workarounds all the time. I have seen people share tools with one another when they could not get what they needed (on a construction site, we had only one T-nailer), purchase a tool themselves (an employee purchased an inexpensive printer for his desk), and adapt tools for uses outside their intended functions (using Microsoft Word to create a slide presentation). These types of workarounds help employees to be productive in the absence of the tool or resource they need. However, to drive exemplary performance, it is best to have the actual tool or resource. Table 8 contains some examples of creative workarounds to give you an idea of how this particular tool can be useful.

The creative workarounds listed in table 8 on the following page are just examples of how you can address a tools and resources issue in situations where you are unable to obtain the identified tool or resource. This table is meant to underscore how tools and resources issues can often be addressed with some creative and strategic thinking.

LEVERAGING THE EXEMPLARY STRENGTH

Many of the tools that can be used for developing an expandable strength related to the tools and resources factor can also be used to leverage an exemplary strength. Often, the process of determining whether tools and resources are the key reason for an exemplary strength will point to the exact tool you will leverage. For example, you and the employee may have determined that her exemplary strength in learning about a prospective client's business is because of information available from her subscription to a business research Web site. Knowing this, you would leverage this resource and provide access to the site for all your salespeople. The key is to determine the tool that is used in a unique way to drive the exemplary strength. Once you do that, you will know what to leverage.

TABLE 8 **Examples of Creative Workarounds**

TOOL OR RESOURCE	SITUATION	CREATIVE WORKAROUND
Client meeting space (Equipment)	Dave doesn't have a private office that can accommodate client visits, so he meets clients at a local coffee shop, where it can be hard to find a seat and the noise level is high.	Dave's boss can't give him an office, but he talks with the training department, and they allow him to schedule time to meet in one of their rooms when it is available.
Access to people	Tia is unable to get timely price quotes to potential customers because her boss, who approves price quotes, spends most of the day in the field and cannot respond quickly.	Tia's boss cannot be present in the office more, but the company gets her a PDA so Tia has real-time access to her boss whenever she needs her to approve a price quote.
Equipment	Matt's computer is too slow to efficiently run the graphic design software he uses once a month to edit the department newsletter.	Until a new computer can be purchased, Matt's boss gives him access to her high-speed computer for two hours on Friday mornings while she attends a meeting of senior managers.
Financial resources	Denelle's team is overworked, and she doesn't have the funds to hire another person to help with the workload.	Denelle is able to get someone from another department to help for four hours a week.

Responsibility for Addressing Tools and Resources

When it comes to developing an expandable strength that is driven largely by the tools and resources factor, both leaders and employees must play a role. Employees have the responsibility to communicate their needs to leaders and to proactively seek out required tools and resources that can be secured on their own (within company policy). In turn, leaders are responsible for helping employees get the tools and resources they need and offering support as the employees work through the process of obtaining the necessary tools and resources. For example, a leader might provide assistance in obtaining additional resources for a job (e.g., adding a staff member, hiring a consultant, or putting in a request for more project funding), or the leader might focus on helping to remove roadblocks related to tools and resources that the employee faces (e.g., changing a policy that gets in the way of effectively doing one's job, talking with another leader to secure direct access to that leader for the employee, or getting updated software so that the employee's computer doesn't crash).

There are also some cases in which employees themselves make an adjustment to tools or resources to improve their own performance. When they do so, they are self-assessing. When an employee gains the ability to self-assess accurately (note that self-assessment is often a by-product of the Exemplary Performance Model), he or she can determine which tools and resources are needed to perform at the exemplary level. For example, as part of the process for developing exemplary performers, I was recently talking with a sales engineer about an exemplary strength she had for conducting demonstrations of one of my company's products. Unlike every other salesperson and sales engineer, who scheduled two hours for the demonstration, she would schedule two and a half hours for the demonstration. That is, she allotted a greater amount of her resource of time to the task than other sales engineers. By adding a half hour to the schedule for the presentation, this sales engineer ensured that she would have ample time to conduct the demonstration and fully answer all of the prospect's questions if the standard two hours wasn't enough. After learning this information, the sales engineer and I were able to leverage this strength to help others improve their performance (i.e., we encouraged them to schedule an additional half hour for their presentations). Although leaders are often responsible for providing employees with the additional tools or resources they need, as this example reveals, employees sometimes find their own opportunities to adjust their tools and resources.

Using the Model in the Real World

To illustrate how the tools and resources factor operates, let me recount a story.

It was an uncharacteristically cold day in Orlando. A cold front had made its way farther south than expected and had caught me off guard. At the time, I was 250 miles from home and didn't have a jacket. The client I was working with was a Fortune 150 home builder. I was working with the client to develop sales training for the people the company had hired to sell the homes they build. The second day I was in Orlando, we went into the field for six hours so that the participants of the training class could practice selling a model home. In that particular community, the models had not been finished, so there were not any customers coming in yet. This was good for role playing. However, there was also no heat, which is terrible for someone caught in cold weather who didn't bring a jacket.

My role was to observe what was done, to document it, and then to write training based on the most effective sales process we could create. By the end of the day, I had taken only a few notes. Fortunately, this was not too much of a concern because I was going to return with the group to the model home the next day so that they could practice again.

That evening in the hotel, I pondered my performance earlier in the day through the lens of the Exemplary Performance Model. I really didn't feel as though I had displayed any exemplary strengths. (Thank goodness performance is judged over time and not on the basis of one occurrence.) However, in seeking my main expandable strength that day, I concluded that it was effective note taking. In other words, my note taking had the potential to be developed from at-standards to exemplary. I chose to focus on developing this strength because doing so would have a great impact on my performance and was important to my ability to achieve the outcomes I was trying to accomplish (i.e., to develop sales training). In thinking about why I didn't take good notes that day, I realized that it was because I was cold and uncomfortable. This discomfort distracted me and took my attention away from what I was supposed to be doing: taking notes that I could use in improving the sales process and in creating training based on the new process. On the basis of a quick review of the performance factors, it seemed, then, that either environment (the cold) or tools and resources (a jacket) was the key performance factor. If I wore a jacket to the site, the cold air wouldn't bother me, and I could take notes. Thus, the performance improvement potential really rested with the tools and resources factor. The environment didn't need to be changed to develop my performance; my tools needed to change. So I went to the mall, found a jacket, and purchased it. The next day I took great notes, which in turn allowed me to discover specific behaviors of the salespeople that could be improved and that could form the basis for sales training that was highly effective. Although this example is a simple one, it demonstrates the way in which the model can help you discover whether the key factor constraining performance is tools and resources.

Conclusion

Addressing a tools and resources issue can be straightforward and simple: upgrade an employee's computer, purchase a cell phone, or buy a new jacket, for example. In cases where organizational constraints prohibit you from obtaining an identified tool or resource, you can often generate creative workarounds to leverage or develop the targeted strength. If you can't afford new cell phones for all your employees, perhaps you can purchase a smaller number of cell phones that can be signed out when employees go out into the field. If an employee's computer can't be upgraded until next quarter, perhaps the information technology department can reconfigure the computer to run more quickly. Some tools and resources challenges will be greater than others, but with some ingenuity and strategic thinking, you can often connect employees with the tools and resources they need to improve performance to the exemplary level.

6

The Systems and Processes Factor

For nearly every task that you accomplish at work, there is a set of steps (often automatic) that make up that task. When you call a client, you probably open your electronic address book to locate the client's phone number; next, you pick up the phone and dial the phone number; then, when prompted by the operator, you ask for the client's extension number; and, finally, when the person answers, you begin your conversation. That's four steps to complete the task of making a phone call. Of course, most of us don't think of the steps of a given task—especially something as simple as a phone call; we simply do the steps automatically. Yet when developing performance, you as a leader will often find it useful to break down the steps required to accomplish a given task so as to identify whether the *process* of accomplishing that task is having an effect on performance outcomes.

The systems and processes factor relates to how things get done at work.

Systems and Processes Defined

The systems and processes factor relates to *how things get done at work*. Specifically, *process* refers to the series of steps a person goes through to complete a task or fulfill a key responsibility, whereas *system* refers to the series of processes people go through to complete a task or fulfill a key responsibility. Systems are needed to achieve more complex outcomes than processes. For example, one system used by a banking organization is the account acquisition system. For this system to work, there are many processes involved. First, the bank must go through the process of developing a specific product (type of account, rules and policies for the account, etc.). Then the product must be advertised. Employees must be trained about the specifications of the account, such as who can open this type of account, how a customer can use it, and how the customer can set it up. After that, the employee goes through the process of selling and setting up the account for customers. As you can see in this example, a system involves many processes (that often occur across departments), many people within an organization, or even many people across organizations (such as when suppliers are involved).

Systems

Examining systems will help you to better understand performance at the organizational level rather than at the level of the individual. As a result, you should use the systems part of the systems and processes factor to improve departmental, functional, or organizational performance. Because my focus in this book is on developing performance at the level of the individual rather than at the level of the organization, I will not focus in this chapter on the systems portion of the factor. Instead, I will explore the meaning, importance, and relevance of *process* to individual performance.

Processes

Again, process refers to the series of steps a person goes through to complete a task or fulfill a key responsibility (i.e., to achieve a specific outcome). Process answers the questions "How do I get my work done?" and "What are the steps that allow me to complete my assigned tasks, to fulfill my key responsibilities, and to achieve my desired outcomes?" Process also captures the order of the steps needed to get work done.

When we hear the word *process* in the context of work, most of us tend to think of processes as being uniform, regardless of who is doing them. However, there are countless work processes that are individualized. The process one person engages in to give a presentation, for example, might vary quite a bit from the process used by another person to give a presentation. In many cases and for many tasks and key responsibilities, process is typically left to the individual employee to design and determine. Only a small percentage of tasks and key responsibilities are achieved using formal, company-designed processes.

FORMAL AND INFORMAL PROCESSES

Formal processes are those that a company has designed to ensure that each employee is engaging in identical steps to fulfill a given task or key responsibility, whereas informal processes are those that individuals develop on their own to complete certain tasks or key responsibilities. Individuals engaging in the same task or key responsibility might happen to design a similar process, but they are just as likely to develop informal processes that vary from one another. If processes (whether formal or informal) are designed well, they will help employees achieve high performance; if they are designed poorly or with flaws, processes may actually impede employees from performing well.[1] Table 9 presents a comparison of what are typically formal versus informal processes at work.

There are pros and cons to using formal and informal processes. The pros of a formal business process include consistency, the ability to measure performance outcomes, and the knowledge that changes in the process have an impact on the outcomes. The pros of an informal business process are that an individual may feel empowered to figure out a better way to accomplish a task and resources are not taken up determining steps for every task. The cons of formal business processes are the amount of time required to determine the steps and the perception by the employee that he or she has to do a task a certain

TABLE 9 **Formal Versus Informal Processes**

TASK	STEPS
Formal process (intended to be uniform for all people)	
Handle a customer complaint	1. Listen to complaint. 2. Restate the complaint to ensure understanding. 3. Communicate what you can do for the customer. 4. Complete a complaint tracking form. 5. Submit form to a manager.
Informal process (can vary for different people)	
Write an agenda for a team meeting	1. Independently brainstorm items to cover. 2. Type items into a new document on your computer. 3. Format the document and proofread. 4. Send the document to the team. OR 1. Send an email to the team to solicit agenda items. 2. Open the agenda template and write the agenda. 3. Save, print, and distribute agenda to the team.

way, even if the person may have an improvement to the process. The cons of leaving the process up to the individual and allowing an informal business process include lack of consistency, disengagement from others on the team, and difficulty in comparing a process among team members.

In sum, you will find that process is the key performance factor for the targeted performance area if the process itself is responsible for the exemplary or expandable strength, rather than the way that the em-

**WHEN COMPANY RULES CONFLICT
WITH COMPANY PROCESSES**

Rules play a role in whether and how employees are able to engage in formal processes. Unfortunately, employees are sometimes forced either to follow specific processes and break a given rule or to alter processes so as not to break the rule. A process that forces someone to violate a rule could mean that the process is bad or that there may be conflicting rules. For example, if my company's customer service process includes asking the customer how I can remedy the situation and then immediately implementing the desired solution, there are probably rules determining what I can do, such as refunding up to 50 percent of the purchase price of an item to the customer. Yet if there is another rule that customer complaints must get solved during the first contact with a customer and the customer wants a full refund, I am put in a situation where one of the rules must be violated (i.e., I refund more than 50 percent) or the process must not be followed (i.e., I don't immediately remedy the situation but instead talk to my supervisor and then call the customer back). When rules conflict with processes, the solution involves either changing the rules or changing the process.

ployee *engages* in the process. For example, if the person doesn't know how to engage in one or more of the steps of the process, this may be an indicator of lack of skills and knowledge. If the person knows how but can't perform the step, this discovery will point to the talent and fit factor. If the person resists in engaging in one particular step of the process, the factor at play could be motivation. In these examples, the process itself is not flawed or broken; instead, the employee is having trouble following the process to the letter owing to a performance factor other than process.

Is the Process Factor Key to an Expandable Strength?

The following questions will help you assess whether process is the key factor responsible for the gap between current performance and exemplary performance for the targeted expandable strength.

1. Does the employee consistently follow a process when completing the targeted task?

2. Does the employee use a process that is different from the process used by an exemplar?

3. Does the recommended process appear to be broken or faulty?

DOES THE EMPLOYEE CONSISTENTLY FOLLOW A PROCESS?

Note that this first diagnostic question is intended to assess two different things:

A. Is a process followed by the employee each and every time the task is done?

B. If so, is the exact same process (same steps, same order of steps) used?

If the answer to either of these subquestions is no—indicating that the employee (a) isn't following a process (series of steps) every time a task is completed or (b) isn't following the *same* process every time—then it's possible that the process factor is the key one constraining performance from becoming exemplary. There could be many reasons why a person is not following a process—reasons that point to other performance factors than process—so you will want to determine whether it is process or one of the other factors that is at play. In particular, you can also use the process of elimination and pose the questions for each of the other factors to help determine whether the process factor or another factor is at play.

Exemplary performers have often discovered the best way of doing something (the best process) and are able to sustain consistent exemplary performance over time because they follow this best way of doing something on every single occasion that they engage in a task. This first diagnostic question thus helps you determine not only whether a person is following a process but, if she does, whether she follows the exact same process every time—important diagnostic data that you will want to capture since doing so is a prerequisite of exemplary performance.

DOES THE EMPLOYEE USE A PROCESS THAT IS DIFFERENT FROM THAT USED BY THE EXEMPLAR?

Process may be the key performance factor for a given targeted expandable strength if the employee has adopted an informal process that is less optimal than the process used by an exemplar in the organization or industry.

If you determine that the answer to this second question is yes—that the employee follows a process that is different in part or in whole from the process used by someone performing the task at an exemplary level—this departure is a sign to dig deeper. In doing so, you will want to determine whether process is the key performance factor for the expandable strength, since it is possible that the employee is not following the process of exemplary employees because of other performance factors outside of process. To check for this possibility, you can run through the questions for the other factors to identify whether one of these factors provides a more compelling reason for the expandable strength. For example, you may find that there are not clear expectations around using a specific process but that helping an individual map out and use a process is a more effective goal than simply providing clear expectations. By asking these questions, you will have useful data for determining whether process is a key factor responsible for the expandable strength.

DOES THE RECOMMENDED PROCESS APPEAR TO BE BROKEN OR FAULTY?

By definition, a faulty process will hold performance back from reaching its fullest potential. For example, if a formal process for arranging for customer seating at a restaurant has been established (e.g., efficient seating of customers in their preferred locations) but this process involves gathering numerous pieces of information from customers and entering this information into a database, the time it takes to complete these process steps might detract from the goal of exemplary customer service. Thus, if you detect that one or more steps in a current process are holding an employee back from achieving exemplary performance for the targeted task, it is likely that process would be a useful factor to target (i.e., by adjusting and improving the company's process).

Determining Whether Process Is the Key Enabler for the Exemplary Strength

As always, the process for determining the key performance factor driving the exemplary strength consists of the following steps:

- Scan the performance factors in the model to see if one factor for the given task stands out to both you and the employee as occurring to a greater degree or in a different form for the employee than for nonexemplary performers.

- If more than one factor is detected, work with the employee to narrow the probable factors to the one factor believed to be *most responsible* for exemplary performance.

In support of this process, you can first ask question 1 for expandable strengths to make sure that the exemplary employee does in fact follow a process consistently.

1. Does the employee consistently follow a process when completing the targeted task?

   If the employee does, and she likely will, since consistent process can contribute to high performance, you can keep process in the running as the possible key performance factor. You can continue to the second question to gain further clarity into the role that process may play in the exemplary strength.

2. Is the process used by the exemplary employee superior to the process used by others?

   To answer this second question, your goal will be to outline the process used by the exemplary employee and then compare it to other, nonexemplary employees' processes to see if a difference exists. If one does, take some time to assess whether this difference seems to enable the exemplary employee to perform at a higher level than the others. If it does, it's quite possible that process is the driver for exemplary performance of the targeted task. Of course, an answer of yes to question 2 does not rule out other factors being more influential on exemplary performance, so you will want to be sure to examine all of the other factors to see if they also seem to play a role in the exemplary strength.

Tools to Target Performance
Related to Processes

There are a few key tools to use when the process factor is determined to be the reason for an expandable strength. As you will see, these tools can also be used to leverage an exemplary strength.

DEVELOPING AN EXPANDABLE STRENGTH

When process is the key performance factor, the tools used to leverage the targeted strength all involve examining the steps people take when engaging in a task or key responsibility and identifying the order in which these steps are completed or should be completed (i.e., identifying the process). For an expandable strength, the goal of the selected tool(s) is to identify the steps taken to accomplish a task or key responsibility and then determine whether there is a better set of steps (process) that could be used, one that would yield increased performance. In particular, are steps missing from the employee's process? Or are needless steps present? Once these questions are answered, you can create an action plan aimed at determining and engaging in the most effective process for the chosen task.

Process Improvement

Process improvement is a procedure in which a given task is broken into its component steps. These steps are then analyzed and can be measured. Responsibilities can be assigned, time frames for each step can be determined, triggers and drivers can be established, and outcomes can be analyzed. By breaking down a process to this level of detail, you may find it clear both why the targeted performance area represents an expandable strength and how to improve or reengineer it. For example, if you were to examine the steps involved in the process of entering payroll information into a computer software program designed for this task, you might find that there is a specific step of transferring hours from a printed report into the payroll program. If this step of the process is not done right, the process error will have an impact on the accuracy of the payroll data, which means that people will be paid incorrectly. Mapping out the process and discovering that this is the area that accounts for the mistakes being made will help

TABLE 10 **Process Improvement in Action**

STEP	DESCRIPTION	EXAMPLE
Break task into steps	List each step that is followed when engaging in the task. The list should reflect how things are currently done.	When bagging groceries do the following: 1. As groceries are being passed down to you, separate into groups: cold items, fragile items, toxic items, and other items. 2. Ask the customer if he or she would like paper or plastic bags. 3. Using boxed items, form walls on each side of the bag. 4. Put the appropriate type of item in the bag (cold items together, toxic items separate from everything else, etc.).
Analyze and measure steps	Determine the effectiveness of each step and measure outcome of step as appropriate. Also examine the impact of each step on other steps.	Separation of groceries is done with 89.49% accuracy, based on an average of those sampled. Proper separation also results in faster bagging of groceries.
Assign responsibility	Determine who is responsible for each step.	Step 1: Joint responsibility between the bagger and cashier. Step 2: The bagger. Step 3: The bagger. Step 4: The bagger.

TABLE 10 CONT'D

STEP	DESCRIPTION	EXAMPLE
Determine time frames	Determine the average amount of time each step in the process takes to complete.	Step 1: Continuous as groceries are being handed down from the cashier (dependent on volume). Step 2: 3.19 seconds per customer. Step 3: 4.1 seconds per bag. Step 4: 11.7 seconds per bag.
Establish triggers and drivers	Determine what prompts each step in the process to occur and what may affect variability in each step.	Step 1: The cashier handing down groceries prompts separation. This is affected by the speed with which the cashier can scan items and whether the customer has unloaded his or her cart ahead of time. (Triggers) Step 2: Once the cashier has started scanning groceries, the customer can be asked about his or her preference. This is affected by whether the customer is "available" to hear and respond to the question. (Driver)
Analyze outcomes	Measure the desired outcomes to determine the overall effectiveness of the process.	• The current process for bagging groceries has led to a decrease in returns of 18%. • Baggers to finish packing bags by the time the customer completes payment 87% of the time, based on an average of those sampled.

TABLE 10 CONT'D

STEP	DESCRIPTION	EXAMPLE
Revise the process	For key areas where the outcomes are not where they should be, determine whether there is a more effective process.	• Rather than the cashier handing down groceries, prompting the bagger to separate and put them in the appropriate bag, the cashier would hand them down placing dry goods to the left of the bagger, frozen and cold goods in the middle, and toxic goods to the right of the bagger.
Measure results of the new process	Measure the results of the new process to determine overall effectiveness of the process improvement.	• The new process for bagging groceries leads to baggers finishing packing groceries by the time the customer completes payment 97% of the time, based on an average of those sampled.

you isolate the reason for an expandable strength and improve the process. See table 10 for more on how process improvement works.

Note that in your initial analysis to determine whether the process is the reason for the particular type of strength (step 2 of the model: diagnose cause(s) of performance), you will stay at a shallower level than when process mapping, simply defining each step and your perception of its effectiveness. In some cases, you will be able to gather metrics to support your perception. In others, you will have to use your judgment. If you suspect that the cause of the strength's being exemplary or expandable is most attributable to this factor, you may then create an action plan to launch a formal process-mapping initiative, getting specific about the components of the process.

Six Sigma

Six Sigma is a data-driven, systematic approach to process improvement that attempts to define, measure, analyze, improve, and control a process.[2] The desired outcome of Six Sigma is a process in which quality measures fall within the parameters of the acceptable levels. Six Sigma guides people to measure the process and make changes until defects are 3.4 parts per million or fewer. The Six Sigma improvement practice requires commitment from the leaders of an organization, specialized training, and statistical analysis of a given process. Because of the time commitment and resources needed, Six Sigma is almost always conducted on more macro processes or systems, that is, processes that span a team, a department, or the organization. However, if Six Sigma is being used in your organization, you may have the opportunity to receive training in conducting a Six Sigma project. If so, and if this tool is chosen as the most appropriate way to develop an expandable strength, you will have the expertise needed to use Six Sigma to examine the process and improve it.

Lean

Also known as "Lean manufacturing," Lean refers to the process improvement methodology of reducing the amount of resources needed to produce a product or the amount of waste generated by its production. This is often done in conjunction with a Six Sigma process improvement project. The focus of Lean is on examining all the processes involved in the creation of a product. However, an individual employee trained in the Lean process can apply the techniques to a product he or she develops. For example, if I am responsible for developing a report that goes to my leader and submitting it on the first Friday of each month, I can apply the Lean process to reduce the time it takes to generate the report, reduce the resources needed, and, at the same time, improve the quality of the report. Therefore, if I had an expandable strength of turning in a report while taking less time to create it, I would be able to use the Lean process as a tool to accomplish this goal.

Quality Awards

Note that one final tool for developing expandable strengths is to pursue quality awards (official honors given to organizations that meet a set of stringent standards for quality). Given that attempting to win a quality award is an organizational initiative for developing performance and will not likely be used to develop the performance of a single employee, I only mention it briefly here.

LEVERAGING THE EXEMPLARY STRENGTH

When the systems and processes factor is the reason for an exemplary strength, the goal during the action plan is to determine which steps are taken by the exemplary employee to achieve exemplary outcomes. Then, you will compare those steps to the steps taken by the typical performer. (If the process is documented, this comparison is easy. However, organizations rarely document processes, except when necessary.) Once you compare the exemplary employee's steps to those of the typical performer, you can see the gap. Does the exemplary employee do something that other employees don't do? Does the exemplar leave steps out that other employees include? Or does the exemplar just engage in some of the steps differently than other employees? Once you determine the answers to these questions, you will be able to see how to leverage the process used by the exemplar and share it with other employees that you manage.

The tools used to develop the expandable strength can also be used to leverage the exemplary strength. Table 11 provides details on how to use each of these tools with the exemplary strength.

As you can see from this table, the tools used to address an expandable strength can also be used to leverage an exemplary strength. These tools allow you to gain better understanding of the process used by the exemplary employee and to capitalize on that understanding so that the process performed by the employee can be adopted by everyone engaging in the identified task. This outcome will reduce variation in the way a process is executed (consistency), have a positive impact on key metrics for the process, and help all employees improve their individual performance of the process.

Responsibility for Addressing Systems and Processes

When it comes to addressing process issues, it is the employee's responsibility to give feedback on making process improvements or mapping out a new process because he or she has valuable insight into what challenges arise when trying to accomplish a certain task or key responsibility. Organizations often err when they try to map out a process without involving the person who conducts the process. Of

TABLE 11 **Tools for Leveraging Exemplary Performance**

TOOL	DESCRIPTION	EXAMPLE
Process improvement	Break the targeted task into its component steps, analyze these steps, and measure them to determine how the process used by the exemplary performer differs from that used by nonexemplary performers.	A restaurant manager may have a process for creating work schedules for his employees that ensures every shift is fully staffed 99.32% of the time. In drilling down into the process, you determine how the manager's process differs from that used by nonexemplary performers.
Six Sigma	Six Sigma process improvement can be used to examine the process for the targeted task to determine how the process used by the exemplary performer differs from that used by nonexemplary performers.	A software developer writes code with 39.86% fewer bugs than the average programmer, so you may use Six Sigma to determine the process she uses, measure the steps in the process, determine the steps that yield exemplary results, change the process used by others, and measure the outcomes of the new process.
Lean	Lean process improvement can be used to examine a process and decrease the amount of resources needed to engage in that process, or the amount of waste produced by the process.	A trainer producing participant guides can examine the process for printing the guides to determine when, why, and how no extra pages are printed and thrown out (0% waste). Knowing this information can help her improve the process of others to eliminate their production of extra pages.

course, the leader typically has the power (or access to the chain of command) to change the process, the information that can help the employee analyze each step in the process, and the knowledge of best practices. Therefore, the leader needs to participate in this effort as well—partnering with the employee to make process changes and bubbling process change requests up the chain of command where needed. Also, if there are legacy policies that interfere with the process and are no longer useful, the leader's role is to work to remove those obstacles.

Using the Model in the Real World

Jack was a supervisor at a telecommunications company and was responsible for overseeing associates who offered telephone service to new and existing customers. When customers decided they wanted to switch from their current phone company to Jack's company, the internal process of doing so involved five different people. For every person involved, there was, of course, a time outlay, such that it took three days to help new customers switch their phone service.

Jack was working with one of his employees when he noticed that his employee was taking a long time to port that customer's phone number (i.e., transfer the phone number from the former company to Jack's company). Although the employee did this within the time frame set by the company, Jack and the employee labeled this task an expandable strength and worked to decipher the key performance factor. The two didn't think it was a talent and fit issue, as the employee performed well in the current environment, was smart and understood the job, and loved helping customers with the establishment of their service. The employee was motivated to do a good job, so motivation was ruled out; he knew the expectations, so clear expectations wasn't the factor; the environment seemed fine; and so on.

Finally, Jack and his employee took a look at the process the employee was going through to port customer phone numbers. They discovered that he was engaging in some redundant steps and that there were inefficiencies and breakdowns caused by the process (e.g., the employee would have to wait for others to respond, and he couldn't move forward until they did). In sum, only the process itself had troubles, not how the employee was engaging in it. They could see that process was the key performance factor, so Jack worked with the employee to come up with a more efficient process. They ultimately redesigned the process to eliminate redundant and inessential steps, and they put some power back into the employee's hands so that the process could now be done by three people instead of five and accomplished in two hours rather than seventy-two. By implementing this process change throughout the entire team, Jack and his employee saved their company $48,000 in the first year.

Conclusion

When you address the process factor of performance at the level of the individual, you gain valuable insight that can be applied for the benefit of your team, your group, or your department. When leveraging an exemplary strength, you will quickly create an action plan for how this process can be shared with other employees to help them increase their own performance. When developing an expandable strength, you will first go through a full cycle of performance development in which you work with an individual employee to redesign the process for his or her optimum performance; as a result, the expandable strength might well become an exemplary strength. In this case, you and the employee can choose to leverage this exemplary strength in the next cycle of the development process, again bringing the benefits of the process redesign to your whole team. As with Jack and his employee at the telecommunications company, vast amounts of time and money can be saved by addressing the process performance factor. Changes begin with the individual, but they are typically enjoyed department-wide.

7

The Clear
Expectations and
Accountability
Factor

Most of us have had at least one of those "oops moments" in our lives when, after putting in a lot of effort on a task or a project, we find out that the results we generated didn't match what someone else was expecting from us. Our reaction can range from frustration to embarrassment to demoralization to anger. When I was younger, I once worked at a drugstore as the head stock person. One day after spending two hours pricing items and setting up a display for a holiday promotion between the greeting cards and the cosmetics, my manager came over and asked what I was doing. He said that he had wanted the display near the front entrance, not in the middle of the store. This was a sure sign that he and I hadn't clarified expectations with each other. In the workplace, as in life, no employee wants to put in a lot of hard work that ultimately gets wasted because the task has to be revisited, redone, or even discarded to better conform to expectations. And most bosses (save for, perhaps, a sadistic few!) don't want to see their employees working hard to gen-

Results that don't align with expectations—that miss the mark—are, by definition, less than exemplary.

erate results that can't be used or that miss the mark of meeting the organization's needs.

As a leader, you must set and communicate clear expectations to your employees. Even when all of the other performance factors are adequately addressed, if expectations are unclear, then your employees will not be in a position to produce exemplary results. Results that don't align with expectations—that miss the mark—are, by definition, less than exemplary. In their book *Developing High-Performance People: The Art of Coaching,* authors Oscar Mink, Keith Owen, and Barbara Mink agree that in a productive culture, "associates know both what is expected of them and how to use feedback to improve performance."[1] And teams that score high on the clear expectations item of the Gallup Q12 employee engagement survey "are more productive, more profitable, and . . . more creative" than those with lower scores on this item.[2] In the next section I will further flesh out each essential component of clear expectations.

Clear Expectations and Accountability Defined

Clear expectations refers to the information you, as a leader, communicate to your employees to let them know the following:

- The outcomes they're supposed to be achieving
- The standards they're supposed to be meeting
- How they are expected to achieve these outcomes
- Why they are expected to achieve these outcomes (how they are helping the organization)
- When they are expected to achieve these outcomes
- Consequences for achieving or not achieving outcomes

Whereas clear expectations need to be given before a task is assigned so that employees know what target they are aiming for in their work, accountability needs to occur after a task has taken place (or was intended to take place) so that employees receive proper feedback in order to improve, know that what they do matters, and know that consequences (either positive or negative) are enforced consistently. *Accountability* refers to the following two components:

- Follow up with the employee to discuss how well he or she is doing at achieving the desired outcomes as prescribed by the clear expectations

- Delivery of the consequences (both positive and, if needed, negative) associated with performance

Clear Expectations

Table 12 provides examples of the clear expectations, relative to a given task, that a leader might provide for an employee.

TABLE 12 **Examples of Clear Expectations**

COMPONENTS OF CLEAR EXPECTATIONS	NURSING TASK: ADMINISTER MEDICATION TO PATIENT	INSTRUCTIONAL TASK: CONDUCT PILOT TEST OF REVISED MATERIALS
Desired outcome	Accurate administration of medication to the patient	Identify items that need to be changed in materials
Standards expected to be met	Administration of proper dose within ten minutes of scheduled time with 99.99% accuracy	Conduct pilot (test) of all training materials conducted before rollout out to intended audience
When outcome is expected	Standard met immediately and maintained throughout employment	Meet standard immediately and maintain throughout employment
How outcome is expected to be achieved	• Dosage calculation • Time management	• Conduct demonstrations • Solicit feedback • Understand and implement quality control for instructional materials

TABLE 12   CONT'D

COMPONENTS OF CLEAR EXPECTATIONS	NURSING TASK: ADMINISTER MEDICATION TO PATIENT	INSTRUCTIONAL TASK: CONDUCT PILOT TEST OF REVISED MATERIALS
Why outcome is expected to be achieved	• To ensure safety of patient • To provide high-quality care of patient • To decrease malpractice liability	• To improve accuracy of materials • To improve quality of materials • To gain stakeholder buy-in
Consequences for achieving standards	• Inclusion of positive performance in monthly performance discussion and annual review • Satisfaction of partial criteria for Nurse of the Year award • Significant contribution to the patient's improved health	• Recognition at team meeting • Inclusion of positive performance in quarterly performance discussion and annual review
Consequences for not achieving standards	• Formal review of performance • Possible disciplinary action	• Performance analysis to discover cause and determine appropriate course of action • Possible disciplinary action

As reflected in table 12, setting and communicating clear expectations will help the employee determine where to focus efforts, what outcomes to achieve, how and when to produce these outcomes, and why these outcomes are significant to the organization. In particular, clear expectations help support positive performance:

- The employee knows what targets to work toward. The employee focuses on what is important to the team or department.

WHAT KINDS OF CONSEQUENCES ARE APPROPRIATE?

Consequences will always support or discourage behavior. For this reason, it is important to make sure that consequences are determined and clearly communicated ahead of time (clear expectations). In doing so, you will delineate both positive consequences for achievement of the desired outcomes and negative consequences for lack of performance. Keep in mind that the nature of the consequence should match the importance of the task. For example, I would not give an employee a day off with pay for completing a weekly report. The level of the reward is far greater than the importance of the task. However, I would recognize the employee at a team meeting if he submitted an accurate weekly report on time for an entire month. Similarly, I would not remove an employee from a project for making an honest mistake on a spreadsheet. Such an error, unless it was deliberate sabotage of the team, could be a learning opportunity for the employee.

- The employee understands his contribution to the success of the team, department, and organization and typically gains motivation from this understanding.

- Clear expectations provide a basis of comparison for self-assessment. That is, the employee can assess how he or she performed in relation to expectations and then drill down into strengths and weaknesses more effectively.

- The employee understands how his performance will be evaluated. Knowing that he will be held accountable to meet performance standards encourages him to work toward the desired consequences and to work to avoid negative consequences.

In contrast, lack of clear expectations can constrain performance because employees are unable to meet standards (or exceed them) if they don't know what is expected of them. When an employee doesn't know what targets to work toward, how he contributes to the organization, or how his performance will be evaluated, he will find it difficult if not impossible to know where to focus his efforts and how he is doing. I have seen people in this situation simply flounder, assume they are doing well, or even leave the organization. This emphasis on clear expectations is reflected in Lee Roy Beach's work: two of the six commitments noted by Beach as necessary for effective management are understanding expectations and presenting clear performance standards.[3]

I once had an experience that illustrates the importance of getting clear on the expectations for a job before you begin.

> *I once worked as a sales trainer for a large organization. I began by filling out the required paperwork, meeting my teammates, and meeting the supervisors and managers in the department I was to work with. Over the course of a few days, I gained insight (through interactions and conversations) into the expectations for me, but I noted with confusion that these expectations differed between my department leaders, my direct boss, and my peers. The department leaders wanted me to start conducting sales training the next week. My boss wanted me to conduct a needs assessment and design a half-day class to meet the identified gaps in skills relative to sales. My teammates wanted me to get to know them and the work they did before I went off and did something.*
>
> *Without clear expectations that everyone agreed on, I would not have been successful, so over the next few days, I focused on clarifying expectations. I met with my boss first and discussed my concern over varying expectations. She then met with the department director and came to an agreement on what would be expected of me for the first few weeks of my sales training job (i.e., desired outcomes such as determining development needs and designing the first module of sales training). We then met with the rest of the training team and let them know of the agreement. Once expectations were clear as to what I was supposed to be doing, I moved on to discuss standards, goals, time lines, and consequences (refer back to table 12 for examples) with my boss. This information provided a clear picture of the expectations for the work I'd be doing and set me up for success. Without these clear expectations, I would have had too many targets to be successful at meeting them all.*

Note that what may seem like clear expectations to you may not be clear to your employees. First and foremost, clear expectations are about signaling and getting buy-in for desired outcomes. Your goal as a leader is to make sure that your employees are aiming to achieve the same desired outcomes that you expect them to achieve. You can achieve buy-in in a variety of ways. For example, you can share your expectations at a performance development meeting and then ask the employee to summarize these expectations for you so you can make sure understanding has occurred. Or you can write expectations down and have the employee read and discuss them with you. Understanding will also be fostered by specific rather than general statements of expectations (as reflected in table 12). You don't need to inform your employees of each step they should take to achieve a task, but specific language (e.g., "hold a coaching discussion with each employee at least once a month") can be far superior to general statements (e.g., "coach employees").

Clear expectations are critical to performance. While working as a sales trainer at an organization, I once arrived at work on Monday and was called in to my boss's office. He spent the next hour writing me up for not following up on a sales contest he had held on the previous Friday. Since Friday was my day off, and he had never before held a sales contest, I didn't know to check the newsletter to find out about the contest and to follow up and reward the winner with his or her prize. You can imagine how it felt to not only be told I did something wrong but to have something in writing in my record when I had no idea of what I was supposed to do. A better way to handle this would have been for my boss to examine the "why" behind my performance. If he had done this, he would have discovered that a lack of clear expectations was why I hadn't produced the desired outcome. As it turns out, he had never set the expectation that he was going to conduct contests on my day off and that I was to follow up on his contests. Simply setting that expectation would have caused me to check the daily newsletter to see if a contest was to be held on my day off and, if he was the one conducting the contest, follow up with the winner. My performance would have been greatly improved.

TABLE 13 **Examples of Accountability**

COMPONENTS OF ACCOUNTABILITY	ACCOUNTING TASK: AUDIT MONTH-END FINANCIAL RECORDS	FLIGHT ATTENDANT TASK: CONDUCT SAFETY TRAINING DEMONSTRATIONS
Follow-up to discuss how well expected outcomes are being achieved	• Review timeliness of audit. • Review accuracy of audit.	• Review accuracy of demonstrations. • Review quality of demonstrations. • Review frequency of demonstrations.
Delivery of consequences	Provide employee with positive consequences (e.g., fulfillment of criteria for bonus) for achieving desired outcomes or negative consequences (e.g., formal review of performance) for lack of performance.	Provide employee with positive consequences (e.g., recognition at a team meeting) for achieving desired outcomes or negative consequences (e.g., documented performance discussion to discover cause and what to do about it) for lack of performance.

Accountability

Table 13 provides some examples of how a leader might provide accountability for specific assigned tasks.

In sum, accountability involves the actions you take as a leader to follow up on the expectations that have been set for the employee (asking how the employee is meeting expectations) and delivery of the consequences previously designated for meeting or missing these expectations.

Accountability helps support positive performance because:

- People are motivated to meet expectations when they know they will receive the positive consequences promised for meeting those expectations and that rewards will not be forgotten.

- People are motivated to perform so that they don't have to experience negative consequences.

As you may notice, there can seem to be a bit of overlap between the clear expectations and accountability factor and the motivation factor. To determine whether motivation or clear expectations and accountability is the factor most responsible for performance, you will need to drill down to the root cause of the performance (why is the strength exemplary or expandable?). If you find an individual is not motivated because of boredom or a shift in the type of work she wants to do, motivation would be the key factor to focus on. If, however, you find that an individual is not motivated because she doesn't know what is expected of her, the root cause of her motivation is really a lack of clear expectations. Knowing the root cause will help you apply the right factor to the identified strength.

In addition, *consistently* administering accountability ensures fairness among team members so that those who work hard see that they get rewarded while those who don't work hard get negative consequences. This kind of fairness is needed by high-performing people.[4] They want to know that the people who don't work as hard as they do or who don't contribute to the goals of the team are not allowed to slide, and that all those who work hard will experience the positive consequences of their efforts.[5]

In contrast, lack of accountability can hurt performance:

- If you don't hold people accountable, even if they know the standards, they may not feel obliged to live up to the standards.

- If employees see that others aren't being held accountable, they may not feel accountable themselves. Consistently holding team members accountable tells every employee that good performance matters and will be recognized.

For example, the health care world is currently experiencing a significant shortage of nurses, who are in high demand. In one hospital, poorly performing nurses were not being held accountable because the prevailing attitude was "We really need them; let's just let poor performance slide." The result was that the high performers became de-

ACCOUNTABILITY VERSUS PUNISHMENT

Note that the goal of accountability is not to punish employees but instead to motivate them to perform well. For this reason, all of the tools noted later in this chapter for fostering accountability are intended to provide a positive method of establishing clear expectations and holding people accountable rather than punishing them. Although some of the consequences of accountability can be deemed "negative" (e.g., an employee not receiving a promotion, not getting to participate in a leadership program, or being told his or her performance level needs to increase to avoid discipline), the goal is not to make employees feel punished, shamed, or demoralized; the goal is to help them build on a strength and feel motivated to perform at a higher level. Accountability motivates, while punishment often has the opposite effect.

moralized by working in this low-accountability environment, and they ended up leaving.[6]

In sum, accountability plays a key role in performance because it serves as a positive reinforcer of desired performance (you notice and respond to positive performance) and a potential disincentive for below-standards performance. When accountability is absent, positive performance goes unrewarded and below-standards performance goes uncorrected.

Is the Clear Expectations and Accountability Factor Key to Developing an Expandable Strength?

When working to determine whether the clear expectations and accountability factor is the key factor for the targeted expandable strength, you will want to examine whether expectations have been given to the employee and whether she has the same expectations that you do. In addition, you will want to examine whether assigned tasks and clear expectations are followed up with accountability measures (e.g., check-in meetings to assess progress, enforcement of positive and negative consequences). The following questions can be helpful in assessing whether clear expectations and accountability represents the key performance factor responsible for holding the targeted strength back from exemplary performance.

1. Have clear expectations been described for the employee?

2. Are the expectations of the employee and leader the same?

3. Is the employee consistently held accountable for performance?

HAVE CLEAR EXPECTATIONS BEEN DESCRIBED FOR THE EMPLOYEE?

When assessing whether this factor is a major contributor to the targeted performance area, take some time to consider first whether expectations have ever been communicated to the employee. Were they spelled out for the given task before the employee began working on it? Remember, setting clear expectations involves discussing the following:

- The outcomes the employee is supposed to be achieving

- The standards the employee is supposed to be meeting

- How the employee is expected to achieve these outcomes

- Why the employee is expected to achieve these outcomes (how the employee is helping the organization)

- When the employee is expected to achieve these outcomes

- Consequences for achieving or not achieving outcomes

So when inquiring whether clear expectations have been given, ask yourself if *all* of the components of clear expectations have been discussed with the employee. In particular, reflect on whether you have spent time with the employee going over his or her job profile, the metrics that will be tracked, standards to meet, goals, time lines, and consequences. If not, this factor may be the key one related to the given expandable strength. If an employee does not know the exact target he or she is supposed to be working toward, it will be impossible to achieve exemplary performance. This would be a critical gap that you would want to remedy before moving on to another factor. Of course, clear expectations and accountability might be only one of several factors affecting performance, so you will want to review all of the other possible factors as well to assess which one is having the *greatest* impact on performance.

ARE THE EXPECTATIONS OF THE EMPLOYEE AND THE LEADER THE SAME?

Even if you have indicated the expectations for the given task to the employee, for any number of reasons, the employee may have formulated a different understanding of these expectations than you've intended. This second question will help you detect whether the employee's expectations align with your own expectations and those of the organization. By asking this question, you will be investigating whether or not you and the employee share the same perception about desired performance. This is the "clear" part of this factor. If you determine that you and the employee do not share the same perception, this factor may be the key one related to an expandable strength.

IS THE EMPLOYEE CONSISTENTLY HELD ACCOUNTABLE?

In addition to the first two questions, which focus on clear expectations, you will want to ask whether accountability measures have been carried out with the employee. Have you followed up with the employee and made clear the designated positive or negative consequences to reinforce the desired outcomes? Again, if not, you may have found the key performance factor responsible for an expandable strength.

However, it's not enough to supply positive or negative consequences occasionally, when you have time, when you remember, or when the opportunity presents itself. Accountability must be delivered consistently. By always following through on your agreement to supply positive consequences for desired performance and negative consequences for not achieving desired outcomes, you create a work climate where accountability is certain. If consistency of accountability is lacking, this may be the key reason that the employee is not yet achieving exemplary performance.

Is the Clear Expectations and Accountability Factor Key to Developing an Exemplary Strength?

In reality, neither clear expectations nor accountability will serve as the key driver of exemplary performance, so you can rule this factor out when looking at exemplary strengths. Although clear expectations or accountability can help a person transform an expandable strength into an exemplary strength (see "Using the Model in the Real World" at the end of this chapter for an example) because they are prerequisites for exemplary performance and can be the missing link to exemplary performance, you are not going to find that the factor most responsible for the exemplary level of performance is clear expectations or accountability. There is a ceiling to how much clear expectations and accountability can contribute to performance (more is not better for this factor; for example, too much accountability can lead to micromanaging, which may reduce performance). Because of this ceiling, one of the other performance factors will likely play a much larger role in driving performance than does the clear expectations and accountability factor.

Tools to Address the Clear Expectations and Accountability Factor

There are a number of tools that can be used to develop the targeted performance area when the key factor is clear expectations and accountability.

DEVELOPING AN EXPANDABLE STRENGTH

Although some of the following tools may be used with other factors, they also apply to situations where clear expectations and accountability is the key factor for developing an expandable strength.

Communication of Information

One of the simplest and most straightforward tools you can use to develop an expandable strength for which the clear expectations portion of this factor is primarily at play is simply to take some time to communicate clear expectations to your employees: the outcomes they're supposed to be achieving, the standards they're supposed to be meeting, how they are expected to achieve these outcomes, why they are expected to achieve these outcomes (how they are helping the organization), when they are expected to achieve these outcomes, and the consequences for achieving or not achieving outcomes. You can cover in this discussion things like the organization's vision, mission, and strategy and goals for the organization, department, and team. These items help people understand the big picture and how they fit in and contribute to the success of the department and the organization.

Feedback
Another tool to address the clear expectations and accountability factor involves providing feedback: information on past performance that allows a person to improve future performance. Feedback, which can be positive or formative, should be specific to the task you observed and should provide information on what was done and why it was good (if positive) or could be improved (if formative).

For example, using positive feedback, you would let the employee know that in working with the CFO, the employee appeared to be completely prepared, spoke clearly and concisely, and made recommendations that were well thought out. This approach was excellent because it moved the conversation forward faster, the CFO understood the employee's logic and direction without having to ask a lot of clarifying questions. In another example using formative feedback, you would let the employee know that when he used jargon in talking with the customer, the customer did not understand what he was talking about. In the future, he might use language the customer can more easily understand or explain exactly what is meant by the industry terminology he regularly uses.

When providing feedback, be specific (e.g., "resulted in three customer compliments") rather than general (e.g., "made a great impact") and stick to sharing facts and observations (e.g., "decreased the customers' level of comfort with you as measured in that section of your customer feedback ratings") rather than making personal attributions (e.g., "you must have rushed people through the call") that could render the feedback ineffective.

Keep in mind that feedback doesn't have to come from you, the leader. You can also set up systems outside of yourself that will provide your employees with feedback. For example, you can actively solicit customer feedback and share it with employees, or you can ask people to self-assess and provide their own feedback. Your role in self-assessment is to ask questions and ensure that employees accurately evaluate themselves.

In sum, by providing feedback, you will show employees that you are paying attention to their performance and are interested in discussing it with them. Providing feedback reinforces that they are accountable for achieving desired outcomes and that you will recognize when they are successful or help them think through how to be more successful in the future.

Coaching

Another tool at your disposal for addressing clear expectations and accountability is coaching, a process that involves helping employees improve performance through determining current performance gaps, assisting them in establishing goals, and providing support toward achieving those goals. When going through this process, employees gain a clearer understanding of what is expected. The coach also holds people accountable for the achievement of goals. Coaching is covered in greater detail in chapter 8.

Competency Models

Another way to address issues of clear expectations is to provide a best-practices list of things a person should do when performing his or her job (i.e., a competency model). The best practices can be (a) general and applicable to the whole organization (e.g., a core competency model for use by all employees); (b) functional and applicable to everyone within a specific area of the business (e.g., sales or customer service); or (c) job-specific (e.g., a nurse practitioner competency model or a software engineer Level 1 competency model). The level of specificity increases as the competency model moves from the organizational level to the job-specific level. Note that the more job-specific the model is, the greater its ability to improve performance. These models help a person understand the desired behaviors, knowledge, skills, and abilities exemplary performers display. They help a person define what the best practices look like.

Job Profiles

As mentioned earlier, a job profile is a comprehensive list of the key responsibilities, tasks, knowledge, skills, abilities, and behaviors required for a particular job. Going over the job profile with an employee and discussing it in detail is a wonderful way to flesh out the organization's expectations for how the employee is to fulfill his or her role and produce desired outcomes. Additionally, a job profile provides a point of reference for accountability. In other words, when reviewing performance with an individual, you can revisit the job profile, review the desired outcomes, and determine where desired outcomes were met and where the employee may still have a ways to go before meeting them.

Goal Setting

Setting specific performance goals (i.e., targets) that are measurable and that must be achieved within a specific time period is another effective way of providing your employees with clear expectations on how and where they should be focusing their energy and on what the desired outcomes are.[7] In addition, having written goals will make it easier for you to follow up with your employees and hold them accountable because you can look at the goals together and assess whether these goals are being met. Note that if you choose to use the tool of providing feedback, as discussed earlier, research has shown that feedback given relative to goals is more consistently associated with performance improvement than is feedback without goals.[8] Goal setting is covered in greater detail in chapter 10.

LEVERAGING AN EXEMPLARY STRENGTH

Although, as discussed earlier, the clear expectations and accountability factor will never be the key driver in leveraging exemplary performance, you can still enlist the exemplary employee for the targeted task in helping others gain clearer expectations and better accountability for that task by using one of the tools for developing an expandable strength. If you find this to be the case, or even that this factor plays *some* role in exemplary performance, you can use those tools to leverage the exemplary strength. For example, you can invite the exemplary employee to coach an employee in a way that provides clearer expectations and better accountability when that has been identified as the key factor for the expandable strength on the same targeted task. Information shared by one's peer in a coaching relationship may be more readily received than that shared by a boss and can be a great way to leverage an exemplary strength of one employee while developing the performance of another.

Responsibility for Addressing Systems and Processes

Employees are responsible for meeting expectations, and leaders are responsible for communicating expectations and holding employees accountable. These responsibilities can be met in a positive way when consequences are clear from the beginning and regular follow-up is scheduled. For example, if you have an employee who is responsible for stocking shelves and he has the standard of having his row of shelves fully stocked by the time the store opens, the employee's role is to work with you to understand performance standards and accomplish the goal of getting his row stocked before the store opens. Your role as leader is to follow up with the employee relative to his goal of achieving this standard.

It is also primarily your role as leader to communicate and clarify expectations. However, this does not absolve the employee from his responsibility to let you know when expectations are not clear. Therefore, the responsibility for the communication of expectations and clarity around expectations is a joint responsibility. This joint responsibility is often reflected in action plans when clear expectations and accountability is the factor most responsible for an expandable strength. The leader will have specific actions, as will the employee.

Using the Model in the Real World

I once gave a presentation to a health care organization and later discovered when evaluating my performance in conversation with our sales associate that I had turned an expandable strength into an exemplary one. Previously, my leader and I had targeted for development my expandable strength of being prepared for presentations. I was already meeting standards for preparation (e.g., by creating my slides, rehearsing the materials, preparing my handouts, and making copies of them), but my leader and I felt that by spending even more time preparing for presentations, I could raise my preparation to the exemplary level (e.g., by having our marketing team edit my slides and handouts to enhance their effectiveness, by rehearsing multiple times, and by conducting a dry run with a small group of employees).

After a presentation a few months later, we reviewed the seven performance factors and discovered that my leader was not regularly checking in on how I was preparing for presentations. We determined that lack of accountability was contributing to my preparation being inconsistent and my strength being expandable rather than exemplary. I wasn't always taking the time to prepare at the exemplary level and therefore didn't maintain that level of performance. Since my leader never held me accountable, I didn't think it mattered that much. So we made an action plan in which my leader agreed to check in regularly with me on how I had prepared for presentations. Because I wanted this follow-up to be a positive experience, I worked hard at preparing, making sure I did everything necessary to perform at the exemplary level. That way, when my leader held me accountable, I could let him know that I had done a great job of preparing by recounting what I had done. And as I improved my preparation, my targeted task of presentation preparation not only became exemplary, but my delivery of presentations improved as well. In particular, I received feedback from four participants indicating that my presentation had been extremely well thought out, that it seemed to flow naturally and seamlessly, and that they were impressed that I didn't need to look at and read my slides.

Conclusion

As this chapter has revealed, clear expectations and accountability drive performance. Clear expectations help drive positive performance because they let employees know what target they are aiming for and thus provide them with the road map needed to align efforts with desired outcomes for the leader and organization. Research also reveals that substantial gains in clear expectations, as measured by the Gallup Q12 survey, "often correlate with productivity gains of 5 to 10 percent, thousands more happy customers and 10 to 20 percent fewer on-the-job accidents."[9] Accountability helps drive positive performance because people are motivated to meet expectations when they know they will receive the positive consequences promised for meeting those expectations—and that those who do not meet expectations will receive the negative consequences designated. Your role as a leader is thus to set clear expectations for your employees and to follow up on those expectations by providing appropriate consequences. By doing so, you will be providing employees with one of the key factors needed to elevate performance.

8

The
Knowledge
and Skills
Factor

One of the best-known and most commonly addressed performance factors is knowledge and skills. Whenever you send an employee to training, you are addressing the knowledge and skills factor, as training is intended to provide the employee with more knowledge or added skills—which, in turn, are expected to increase an employee's ability to perform well. Assuming you've accurately identified the key performance factor as knowledge and skills, sending your employee to training has the potential to yield improvement in performance. (Note that, as discussed in chapter 1, training is all too often used in vain when the factors underlying performance have nothing to do with a lack of knowledge or skills.) In this chapter, I will review what it means to have knowledge or skills and explore how the presence of knowledge and skills can contribute to a person's performance.

Once leaders understand the many possible performance factors and grow familiar with the tools helpful in addressing them, the temptation to turn to training when it's not appropriate will be significantly less.

Knowledge and Skills Defined

The knowledge and skills factor centers around learned behaviors. Knowledge accounts for the learning necessary for performance. Skills account for the ability to engage in specific behaviors needed for performance. As you will see, they are interrelated and dependent on each other in order for a person to be able to perform. In other words, without knowledge, you will not be able to gain the proper skills, and without skills, knowledge is useless.

Knowledge

Knowledge, in the work setting, refers to the facts and information that a person needs to do his or her job successfully. Necessary knowledge for different workers might include generally accepted accounting practices (for an accountant), adult learning theory (for an HR and learning professional), building design principles (for an architect), or the regulations of the Securities and Exchange Commission (for a stockbroker). Knowledge serves as the foundation of performance. That is, knowledge guides the actions a person will take to successfully meet the desired outcomes of his or her job.

For example, an accountant will not be able to balance the monthly departmental budget if she doesn't have knowledge of the accounting practices needed to do so. Similarly, a stockbroker trading oil futures who doesn't stay current on knowledge regarding the geopolitics of international trade and the status of supply and demand won't be able to make effective trading decisions. Another way of saying this is that knowledge is necessary to build the skills needed to do a job.

Skills

Skills are the capabilities needed to do one's job successfully. Unlike talent, which is innate, skills can be learned and developed over time. If you don't have a skill today, with the right training and support, you have the potential to acquire that skill tomorrow. (In contrast, if you don't have the talent to be good at something today, no amount of training and support can give you that talent.) Skill refers to a particular performance ability, such as the ability to use Microsoft Excel (for

WHAT IS THE RELATIONSHIP BETWEEN SKILL AND TALENT?

Although skill and talent are quite different—the former can be taught and developed, whereas the latter cannot be taught and is simply present or not—skill and talent work together to contribute to performance. For example, although having a certain degree of skill can help someone perform a task, talent is typically necessary to increase performance to the exemplary level. In other words, with skills development, a person can become good at a task, but that person probably won't become great at it unless he or she also has talent. In short, talent is a prerequisite to developing exemplary skill (think of the Michael Jordan example from chapter 3). Similarly, a person could have natural talent for a given area of performance, but until that person undergoes adequate skill development, his or her performance will not reach its potential and may fall short of exemplary. For example, someone might have a natural ability (talent) to mentally visualize effective designs for ad copy, but until he has learned how to use graphic design software (a skill), he won't be able to reach exemplary performance as a graphic designer for ad copy.

an accountant), the ability to design interactive and engaging learning experiences (for an HR and learning professional), or the ability to draw building plans (for an architect).

Skills enable individuals to perform. That is, performance itself is made up of a person engaging in a skill or a number of skills to achieve a desired outcome. Conversely, a person who lacks a needed skill simply can't perform. For example, if the administrative assistant for the vice president of marketing is asked to create a spreadsheet detailing the effectiveness of each marketing channel but does not have the skill of using a spreadsheet program like Microsoft Excel, the administrative assistant will not be able to perform. Note that no matter which other performance factors are present—no matter how clear the expectations are, how much motivation a person has, how effective the available tools are, how conducive the work environment is, how effective the process is, or how much talent a person has—a person needs the appropriate skills in order to perform at standards. And to reach the exemplary level of performance, advanced skills are needed *in addition* to each of the other performance factors.

HARD AND SOFT SKILLS

One way to categorize skills is as technical (or hard) skills or soft skills. Technical skills refer to an individual's abilities to perform the functionally required and technical aspects of a job, such as soldering a pipe (for a plumber), using an amortization table (for a mortgage broker), or interviewing a job candidate (for a recruiter). Soft skills refer to an individual's abilities to perform the interpersonal aspects of a job, such as communicating, coaching, or working in teams. The skills factor is often easier to determine for technical skills issues than for soft skills issues. This is because technical skills usually have clear metrics and standards, which make it easier to measure the outcomes and to compare these outcomes to desired levels of performance. Also, the behaviors and processes needed to accomplish a technical skill are more specifically defined than for a soft skill. Again, this makes it easier to detect technical skills than soft skills. For example, to accomplish the technical skill of processing the coinsurance amount collected from a patient, the office manager must determine the amount that is not covered by insurance and charge the amount due to the patient's credit card or collect the proper amount of cash. To determine whether this technical skill is being performed well, a leader can audit the payment books after the office closes each afternoon, checking to determine whether or not the right amount was charged to the patient and the payment was collected in the appropriate manner.

In contrast, soft skills can be hard to detect because the outcome of using these skills is often intangible. For example, an employee's job profile might indicate that the soft skill of effective communication is required for a job, but it might give no concrete metrics for assessing whether the employee is successful at engaging in this skill (the desired outcome). The leader can observe the employee and develop a *subjective* impression of whether the employee is effectively communicating, but there will be no concrete outcomes that can be easily assessed as occurring directly as a result of that soft skill. On the one hand, if an employee is a manager and her direct reports perform poorly, is this a result of ineffective communication by the manager or something else? On the other hand, if the direct reports perform well, is this a result of effective communication by the manager? The answer is unclear because it is difficult to detect concrete outcomes from a soft skill like communication.

WHY IS THE KNOWLEDGE AND SKILLS FACTOR SO COMMONLY CITED?

As noted earlier, the knowledge and skills factor is the first performance factor that leaders tend to look to when addressing performance. One reason for this tendency is that leaders will have an easy "fix" for the performance issue—training—if they peg that issue to lack of knowledge or skills. Another reason for this tendency is that this approach allows leaders to abdicate responsibility for their role in a person's performance. Instead of looking at what leaders can do to develop performance (e.g., provide better tools, adjust the work environment, communicate clearer expectations), leaders often simply recommend the employee-centered solution of getting the person to training. It's sad but true. Still another reason that leaders take this approach is because they themselves lack the knowledge and skills to examine performance at all levels (i.e., consider all possible factors). Once leaders understand the many possible performance factors and grow familiar with the tools helpful in addressing them, the temptation to turn to training (and the knowledge and skills factor) when it's not appropriate will be significantly less.

Is the Knowledge and Skills Factor Key to an Expandable Strength?

There are certain questions you can ask to help detect whether a person is lacking the knowledge or skills to perform at an exemplary level. These questions alone will not indicate whether the knowledge and skills factor is the key performance factor explaining the gap between expandable and exemplary performance, but certain answers to these questions will serve as signals that the knowledge and skills factor might well be playing an essential role in performance and that you should probe deeper to confirm whether this is the case. The diagnostic questions for the knowledge and skills factor are as follows:

1. If the person had to, could he or she perform the task at a higher level than is currently the case?

2. Has the person performed this task at the exemplary level at any time in the past?

3. Will further improvement of knowledge or skills be likely to improve the person's performance?

1. IF THE PERSON HAD TO, COULD HE OR SHE PERFORM THE TASK AT A HIGHER LEVEL?

This question tries to get at the core knowledge and skills issue of *ability*. Phrased a different way and perhaps in cruder terms, if the person had a gun put to his head, could he engage in the specified task at a higher level than is currently the case? Or looked at in a more positive vein, if the person were offered a million dollars, could he engage in the specified task at a higher level? If the answer to this question is no, you may be looking at a knowledge and skills issue. If a person doesn't do a task well when it's a matter of life and death or a matter of gaining a huge reward, there's a good chance that the person simply doesn't know how to do the task well. When we are backed up at the edge of a cliff, most of us will do what we need to do to avoid getting pushed over the edge and will do it to the best of our ability as a sort of insurance policy against failure—unless, of course, we don't have the knowledge or skills necessary to accomplish the lifesaving task.

This gun-to-the-head analogy is, of course, a strange metaphor to apply to the workplace. I don't encourage you to put your employees into life-or-death situations to test this question out! Instead, the idea here is to invite the employee to imagine being in a hypothetical situation where he must accomplish the task well (for whatever metaphorical reason) and to self-assess whether he would be able to perform in such a situation. If he says yes, and if, on the basis of your own observations and understanding of the employee, you agree that the employee is *capable* of performing the task well, you will gain a sense that the employee has the knowledge and skills needed to engage in that task at a high level and that a different factor might be what's holding him back from exemplary performance. For example, the employee might fall short of such performance owing to a toxic work environment, lack of motivation, inadequate resources, or another reason. Ultimately, if you believe the employee is capable of performing at a higher level on the basis of his current repertoire of knowledge and skills, then this factor may not be the key one at play for the expandable strength.

2. HAS THE PERSON PERFORMED THE TASK AT THE EXEMPLARY LEVEL AT ANY TIME IN THE PAST?

With this question, you are trying to assess whether the person has the ability to perform the given task at the *exemplary* level. If, upon reflection and discussion, you and the employee find that he has performed the given task at the exemplary level at some point in the past, then you have evidence that he may have the prerequisite knowledge and skills to perform the task at the exemplary level—and that a different performance factor is what's holding him back from exemplary performance. Once you identify a past situation or situations in which the employee performed at the exemplary level, you will want to investigate further to determine whether this performance was just a fluke that occurred due to good luck or circumstances or whether it could truly be attributed to adequate knowledge and skills. If you and the employee conclude that the performance was due to a fluke or fortunate circumstances, then the key performance factor might still be knowledge and skills (you can't know for sure, but you will want to dig deeper instead of ruling it out). If, on the other hand, the two of you find that the past higher-level performance occurred as a result of adequate knowledge and skills, you can rule out the knowledge and skills factor and inquire as to what other performance factor was present that has not been present when the employee performs at the current level. For example, has the environment changed since that instance of exemplary performance? Has the process of engaging in that task changed? Was the person's level of motivation substantially higher?

3. WILL FURTHER IMPROVEMENT OF KNOWLEDGE OR SKILLS BE LIKELY TO IMPROVE THE PERSON'S PERFORMANCE?

After you've done a sort of process of elimination by asking the previous two questions, you can consider this last diagnostic question. This question is direct and helps you get to the heart of the knowledge and skills issue. When contemplating this third question, your goal is to try to answer whether you and the employee believe that her performance has the potential to increase to a higher level if she acquires additional knowledge or gains additional skills. Of course, the two of you probably won't be able to answer this question with absolute certainty, but the goal here is to hypothesize regarding the expected benefit of adding more knowledge or improved skills to the employee's repertoire. For example, perhaps an employee has the targeted expandable strength of getting vendors to carry your company's night cream. The employee indicates that she doesn't have enough information on the benefits of the cream when compared with other products to effectively persuade vendors to carry it. She realizes that she is at a loss for words when vendors ask her directly, "Why should I carry your cream over your competitor's?" This is a valuable clue that the knowledge and skills factor, specifically the knowledge, is keeping the expandable strength from becoming exemplary. In this case, the employee is able to identify a specific instance in which she lacks knowledge related to the given task, thereby indicating that by addressing this knowledge gap, performance can likely be improved. By asking the direct question of whether you and the employee believe that additional knowledge or skills are needed to develop performance and by thinking through specific instances of expected improvement, you will get at the heart of whether the knowledge and skills factor is at play for the expandable strength.

Is the Knowledge and Skills Factor Key to an Exemplary Strength?

As in the previous chapters, the process for determining the key performance factor driving the exemplary strength consists of the following steps:

- Scan the performance factors in the model to see if one factor for the given task jumps out to both you and the employee as occurring to a greater degree or in a different form for the employee than for nonexemplary performers for the given task.

- If more than one factor is detected, work with the employee to narrow the probable factors to the one factor believed to be most responsible for exemplary performance (i.e., most variant from nonexemplary performers).

Unlike several of the other factors, for the knowledge and skills factor the three diagnostic questions for the expandable strength do not adapt easily to the exemplary strength diagnosis. Instead, the following questions will be helpful in detecting whether knowledge and skills play a key role in the employee's exemplary strength.

1. Does the employee demonstrate significantly greater knowledge than nonexemplary performers regarding the given task?

2. Does the employee demonstrate significantly greater skills than nonexemplary performers in the given task?

These simple questions can help you examine whether the difference between the exemplary employee and nonexemplary employees for the given task relates to a differential in knowledge or skills between the two kinds of employees. If you assess that the person does indeed possess greater knowledge or skills than nonexemplary performers for the given task, this is a signal that the knowledge and skills factor may serve as the key driver of exemplary performance. Of course, multiple factors typically work together to create exemplary performance, so you will want to assess all of the other performance factors as well and spend some time with the employee contemplating which one seems to *most* differentiate the employee's exemplary performance from others' nonexemplary performance for the given task.

Tools to Develop an Expandable Strength

There are a number of tools that can be used to develop an expandable strength that is linked to the key factor of knowledge and skills. These include training, role modeling, researching, coaching, and stretch assignments.

TRAINING

One of the most commonly used tools for addressing knowledge and skills issues, training refers to a structured presentation of activities, lectures, facilitated discussions, or assignments that help a person learn a specific topic or develop a skill related to that topic. Training can be led by an instructor in a classroom in real time (synchronous), recorded and viewed at a later time (asynchronous), created and made available virtually (online or e-learning), or conducted on the job. Those developing an expandable strength could take a training session to increase the knowledge and/or skills needed to engage in a task and perform at a high level.

ROLE MODELING

Role modeling, also called behavior modeling, is simply learning through observation. Role modeling occurs when we observe some- one do something and then emulate that person. When developing an expandable strength, the employee might observe a role model and then practice what he or she learned from that observation. Note that you may or may not actually know the person who is the role model. For example, if I want to improve my golf game, I can look to experts such as Tiger Woods and Phil Mickelson as role models and try to do what they do to help me improve. I don't have to know these men per- sonally to learn from them but can observe their techniques on televi- sion and read about their golf game and then model my own per- formance after theirs.

RESEARCHING

Researching refers to finding information from various sources related to a specific topic. Someone using research to develop an expandable strength might read a book on performance improvement and report findings to his team. Information is available from many sources, such as in books, journals, electronic databases, resources from professional organizations, blogs, chat rooms, news media, and Web sites. One cau- tion: much of the information on the Internet is based on opinions rather than facts. If an employee is using research to develop an ex- pandable strength, make sure you direct him or her to credible sources, whether Internet based or otherwise.

COACHING

Coaching refers to a relationship where one person (the coach) guides another toward the goal of learning or developing a skill. An employee developing an expandable strength could undergo coaching with an exemplary performer for the given task. For example, a leader could seek out another leader who is higher up in the organization's hierarchy to give her guidance relative to hiring the best people for her team. The coach would guide the person through the steps he takes to determine whether or not a candidate for a job opening will be the best fit and has the greatest talent for the job. According to the International Coach Federation:

> Individuals who engage in a coaching relationship can expect to experience fresh perspectives on personal challenges and opportunities, enhanced thinking and decision making skills, enhanced interpersonal effectiveness, and increased confidence in carrying out their chosen work and life roles. Consistent with a commitment to enhancing their personal effectiveness, they can also expect to see appreciable results in the areas of productivity, personal satisfaction with life and work, and the achievement of personally relevant goals.[1]

There are many resources that can help you develop your coaching skills. In fact, an Internet search on the topic yields millions of results. One resource I have found particularly useful is *Coaching for Performance: Growing People, Performance, and Purpose* by John Whitmore. Information on coaching competencies can also be found on the International Coach Federation's Web site (www.coachfederation .org/ICF). Whatever the source, you may want to develop your coaching skills, because coaching can be a powerful tool to help an employee leverage and develop strengths.

STRETCH ASSIGNMENTS

The tool of stretch assignments involves giving a person tasks that are challenging and typically that the person has not taken on before. For example, if an employee had an expandable strength of learning to create a budget, you may assign him the task of creating a budget and then provide guidance to help him learn how to create an effective budget. By doing this, you create a real "deliverable" that the employee is responsible for rather than a contrived role-playing exercise that may not have as much meaning. People tend to learn at a deeper level when this kind of meaning is attached. As the employee works to create a budget, he will have to tie what he is doing to past learning (such as creating a personal budget), ask others how they created their budgets, and get feedback from you. This activity will stretch his abilities beyond what they were before the task was assigned.

Leveraging an Exemplary Strength

The knowledge and skills factor is always present in an exemplary strength. Without it, an employee cannot perform at the exemplary level. However, while it may be present, it may not be the key factor that explains the exemplary strength. As for an expandable strength, you will not want to default to this factor too quickly when you are assessing the key factor for an exemplary strength.

Each of the tools used to develop an expandable strength can also be used to leverage an exemplary strength related to the knowledge and skills factor. Table 14 provides an overview of how each of these tools can be used to leverage the targeted exemplary strength.

Responsibility for Addressing Knowledge and Skills

The responsibility for addressing strengths related to knowledge and skills lies with both the leader and the employee. Because the leader and the employee both have information that may be helpful, both must first determine that this factor most drives the exemplary strength or explains the expandable strength. For example, the leader should share any facts and observations that will help with determining whether this factor is at play. The employee should share his or her information and participate by self-assessing.

If the knowledge and skills factor is determined to be the factor most responsible for an exemplary strength or expandable strength, there are actions both the leader and the employee can take. These measures will be captured in the action plan. For example, both should contribute their ideas on how to leverage an exemplary strength or develop an expandable strength, and both should follow through on their action items. Only through a partnership will the most effective action plan be developed.

TABLE 14 **Knowledge and Skills Tools for Leveraging Exemplary Strengths**

TOOL	DESCRIPTION	EXAMPLE OF A TASK	EXAMPLE OF AN EXEMPLARY STRENGTH
Training	Exemplary performer (EP) conducts special training on how to perform a certain task at the exemplary level.	Shelving books at the library	EP contributes to or leads training on a mnemonic device to remember and better use the Dewey Decimal System.
Role modeling	EP serves as a role model for others in the organization with regard to the given task.	Facilitating a team meeting	In the leader's absence, EP leads the team through all agenda items using team facilitation skills.
Researching	EP shares references supporting the method used to perform a task at the exemplary level.	Involving employees in decisions	EP writes a short paper with specific references on the benefits of employee involvement.
Coaching	EP coaches other employees in a specific performance area related to targeted strength.	Handling a difficult colleague	EP uses questioning, dialogue, and action planning to help an employee develop tactics to handle a difficult situation with a colleague.
Stretch assignments	EP leads someone striving for exemplary performance in doing a task that represents a stretch assignment for the other employee.	Splicing fiber optic cable	EP directs an installation technician who will splice fiber optic cable for the first time.

Using the Model in the Real World

I once worked with a leader of a nonprofit organization. Although she had created a strategic plan once before and had done a good job, because of changes in the organization, she was going to have to do this more frequently and needed to expand this strength. In reviewing the factors, we determined that she had all the other factors accounted for but that there was room for her to increase her skill in this area. In particular, she would not be successful unless she learned how to facilitate a more effective strategic planning methodology and developed greater skill to implement it. We decided that she would observe me conducting a strategic planning session with her team. I would then review the process with her by answering questions and role-playing to help her develop skill. As a result of using the tools of role modeling and coaching, the leader was able to conduct a strategic planning meeting for the team of a colleague and received excellent feedback.

Conclusion

Assessing whether a targeted strength relates most to the knowledge and skills factor can be quite straightforward. For example, if an employee assesses himself or herself as lacking sufficient knowledge or skills to perform a certain task at the exemplary level (in the case of an expandable strength), you can dig a little deeper, confirm that this is the case by asking the questions discussed above, and then select the right tool to address the targeted performance area. If instead you discover knowledge and skills is not the key factor for an expandable strength, you will have saved yourself, your employee, and the organization the expense and frustration of applying the wrong solution.

You must be careful not to default to the knowledge and skills factor when addressing performance. Leaders too often assume that performance will be improved by increasing knowledge and skills. Although this is certainly the case some of the time, before you create an action plan to address knowledge and skills, you want to be sure that none of the other performance factors are what's really at play for a targeted strength. This diligence will pay substantial dividends because you will know you are applying the right tool to develop or leverage the strength.

9

The Motivation Factor

This chapter focuses on the last of the performance factors: the motivation factor. I've saved this factor for last because determining whether motivation is the primary performance factor at play may involve scanning through the other factors first. There is a lot of overlap between motivation and the other six factors, so it's not always clear whether motivation or one of the other six factors is at play. Even if motivation seems

> *You need to ask the right questions to verify whether motivation is the key performance factor or simply a symptom of one of the other factors.*

to present itself as the primary factor, you need to drill down deeper and ask the right questions to verify whether motivation truly is the key performance factor or whether it's simply a symptom of one of the other factors being at play.

Motivation Defined

Motivation, in the context of work, refers to an employee's desire (or drive) to engage in work and achieve results at the step, task, key responsibility, or job level. If the employee wants to achieve results and is interested in doing the necessary work, he or she is motivated. If the employee does not have the desire to achieve results and has no interest in doing the necessary work, he or she is not motivated. Of course, this is a simplified definition. We know that, rather than an employee simply being motivated or not, there are varying degrees of motivation that an employee can experience. For example, one employee may be motivated to do just enough to meet expectations, while another is motivated to perform at the exemplary level.

Motivation comes in two forms: extrinsic and intrinsic.

- Extrinsic motivation refers to a person's drive to accomplish a specific outcome on the basis of a belief that he or she will receive an external tangible reward (such as a financial bonus, a vacation to Hawaii, or football tickets).

- Intrinsic motivation refers to a person's drive to accomplish a specific outcome on the basis of a belief that he or she will experience an internal intangible reward (such as a sense of pride, new knowledge, or personal satisfaction) as a result.

Research has shown that intangible rewards tend to be the most effective motivators, although tangible rewards, if properly selected, can serve as motivators as well.[1] What I mean by "properly selected" is that you choose the right external, tangible motivator for a given person—something that the person you are trying to motivate really cares about (say, Broadway tickets for someone who appreciates culture). The tools offered by the present model cover both categories of rewards: tangible and intangible. Each has its place in motivating employees. (Tangible versus intangible rewards are discussed in greater depth in "Which Rewards Are More Motivating: Tangible or Intangible?" later in the chapter.)

A person's motivation at work (and elsewhere in life) often stems from whether the person values the tangible and/or intangible rewards anticipated for engaging in that work and whether the person considers those rewards to be sufficient. If the rewards anticipated for that work are attractive enough to a person (sufficient and valued), the person will feel motivated to work. If the rewards expected for that work are unattractive (insufficient or not valued), a person will not feel motivated to work. If you have an employee who is unhappy with his pay, who complains that his peers don't value him, or who indicates that his work is not personally rewarding (all references to intrinsic or extrinsic rewards), motivation is likely the key performance factor. In sum, when trying to determine whether motivation is the primary factor for performance, you will want to ask whether the rewards a person receives for doing a job play a key role in contributing to his performance (for leveraging an exemplary strength) or holding him back from still higher levels of performance (for developing an expandable strength).

Motivation as a Symptom Versus a Cause

Given that motivation refers to a person's desire to engage in a certain kind of work (whether at the step, task, key responsibility, or job level), we might assume that anyone who expresses a lack of desire to engage in work is evincing motivation as the key performance factor. After all, when someone says, "I don't want to do X," "I'm not interested in that project," or something similar, we can fairly say that the person doesn't want to do that work (i.e., isn't motivated to do that work). Yet does a lack of motivation (a general psychological concept) mean that the motivation factor (as defined by the present model) is truly the key factor at play?

Whereas motivation as a psychological concept refers generally to *a person's drive to do something,* motivation as a performance factor refers more narrowly to a person's drive to do something on the basis of the belief that *the rewards promised for that work are sufficient and valuable.* Therefore, if someone displays a lack of motivation, although we can say that the person feels unmotivated, we *cannot* immediately assume that the motivation factor is the key one at play. We must first rule out the other six performance factors to make sure that the current feeling of being unmotivated isn't actually a *symptom* of one of the other performance factors.

Actually, motivation plays a role in all of the factors, not just in the motivation factor itself. If you feel clueless about how to do your job (knowledge and skills factor), if you detest your boss (work environment factor), if you feel as though the processes you are required to use are ineffective (systems and processes factor), and so on through all of the factors, you probably will feel unmotivated to do your work beyond what is necessary to keep your job. Yet in these cases, lack of motivation is the *symptom* of another performance factor, not the root cause. You will feel unmotivated to do your work, but it is not so much because of a lack of tangible or intangible rewards (the motivation factor) as it is because of one of the other factors. If the key performance factor (knowledge and skills, work environment, etc.) in each of these cases gets addressed, motivation will likely return.

I've defined the motivation factor more narrowly than the general psychological concept of motivation for two reasons: first, to provide leaders with a more concrete concept of a performance factor than something as general as desire to do work and, second, to differentiate this factor from the other six factors and eliminate overlap

Thus, one can't use the criteria of "desire to do work" to identify which performance factor is at play.

Is the Motivation Factor Key to an Expandable Strength?

To aid our diagnosis of motivation, we can consider the three aspects of expectancy theory by Victor Vroom.[2] Vroom's model is based on three concepts backed by his research: motivation occurs when (1) the anticipated reward is valued, (2) the individual expects that he or she will actually receive the reward, and (3) the individual will be able to perform well enough to receive the reward. These concepts form the basis of the diagnostic questions for developing an expandable strength.

1. Are the rewards for doing a given task valued by the employee and considered to be sufficient?

2. Does the employee feel that there is a high probability of receiving the rewards for doing a given task?

3. Does the employee feel that there is a high probability of achieving the level of performance necessary to receive the rewards?

1. ARE REWARDS VALUED AND SUFFICIENT?

In asking this question, you are really asking about two separate aspects of the reward. First, you are asking whether the reward you are giving is something that the employee desires (or values). For example, if you are giving a cash reward to the top salesperson selling warranty agreements, is money valued by the employee? If so, the reward has the potential to motivate the desired level of performance. Second, you are investigating whether the selected reward is being given in an amount sufficient to motivate the employee to perform at the desired level. For example, is the amount of cash you are offering as a reward to the top salesperson enough to encourage the employee to perform at the desired level? Assuming that the employee does value money as a reward, does the cash reward need to be $50, $100, $500, or $1,000 to motivate the employee to perform?

As discussed earlier, rewards can be tangible or intangible. Tangible rewards refers to such things as pay, movie tickets, and financial bonuses—material things that the company gives to the employee. If your employee indicates dissatisfaction with any of these items, this may be a sign that current tangible rewards are not valued or are considered insufficient by the employee to motivate her to engage in the specified work. Not everyone is comfortable asking for tangible rewards, so you may need to probe a little here to assess whether employees find the current tangible rewards to be valuable and sufficient. If an employee does not mention any of these tangible rewards as a problem, inquire about them directly. For example, you could ask:

- "Are you happy with your pay?"
- "Do you like to go to the movies?"
- "Do you feel your bonus was fair?"

Although you may be reluctant to ask about tangible rewards, through these questions you can gain valuable information in diagnosing whether or not motivation is the key factor for an expandable strength. An answer of no may signal that the motivation factor is the key factor affecting performance.

Of course, tangible rewards are only part of the motivation picture. As noted earlier, research shows that intangible rewards are typically more motivating to employees than are tangible rewards. Intangible rewards are those abstract but nonetheless real items that drive a person's intrinsic motivation, including things like praise, growth opportunities, chances to engage in work that the employee is passionate about, and other rewards that will increase a person's sense of fulfillment. As with tangible rewards, the value of an intangible reward is determined by the individual. An intangible reward that may work for one individual (such as the opportunity to lead a team meeting) might not work for another person (she may feel anxiety around it and not enjoy the experience). When assessing whether internal rewards are sufficient for an employee, you might ask:

- "Do you get personal satisfaction out of the work you do?"
- "Does it make you feel a sense of personal fulfillment?"
- "Do you feel proud of the work you are doing here?"
- "Do you feel you are growing professionally in your job?"

Intangible rewards are difficult to measure because they refer to abstract aspects of someone's internal world: things like contentment, pride, and stimulation. Yet the above questions will provide you with some of the information needed to assess whether the motivation factor is at play. Of course, you will not be assessing the employee's answers to the previous questions in a vacuum; you will be enlisting his or her opinion on the subject as well, which will be extremely helpful.

Note that some employees value and need intangible rewards more than others, so there is no objective measure for how much is enough to intrinsically motivate someone to engage in the given work. Instead, you will want to have a conversation with each employee to determine whether he or she values the intangible rewards given by leaders, peers, and the work itself and whether he finds these rewards to be sufficient. If not, motivation may be the key performance factor at play.

2. IS THERE A HIGH PERCEIVED PROBABILITY OF RECEIVING REWARDS?

The second diagnostic question for the motivation factor asks about the perceived certainty of receiving rewards. The reward associated with performing a given type of work can be valued by and sufficient for an employee; however, if he is not sure that the reward will actually be provided, it will not motivate performance. The converse is also true: if an employee knows he will receive the associated reward, he will feel motivated to engage in the given work.

RULING OUT TALENT AND FIT

It is important to note that an answer of no to the question "Do you get personal satisfaction out of the work you do?" could also point to a talent and fit issue, not just a motivation issue. If you can't tell which is the issue—motivation or talent and fit—try to dig deeper into the issue and find out why the employee is dissatisfied. Does the employee not get satisfaction because she feels she is doing the best she can yet can't get to the exemplary level? This feeling would point to a talent and fit issue. Conversely, does the person not get satisfaction because she is bored with the task and no longer finds it challenging? This feeling would point to a motivation issue. By digging deeper in this way, you will have a better idea of which factor is at play, and you can proceed in drawing up a targeted action plan. And remember that diagnosing the root cause of performance is done in service of creating an effective action plan to target performance, not just for the sake of understanding. So long as you and your employee have come up with an action plan that excites and energizes the employee to develop her performance, you will be on track, and the key factor at play will likely become clear as you observe whether a given action plan yields performance improvement.

For example, consider a small accounting staff that was promised they could end their workday at lunchtime on Friday and be paid for the entire day if they finished processing all accounts payable to the organization with zero errors. The members of the team expressed visible excitement about the promised reward, demonstrating that the reward was valued and sufficient. However, on Wednesday, the director of the Finance Department heard about the contest and called it off. The members of the team felt crushed. They had put in a lot of extra effort to try to attain the goal of zero errors and had ended up receiving nothing for it. Two months later when the leader received permission to hold the contest again, it did not have any impact on performance. When he asked why, he discovered that the team members didn't believe that they would actually get rewarded; they believed that it was just a repeat "scam" to get them to work extra hard for a short time. The group perceived the probability of actually receiving the reward as very low and were not motivated to perform any differently than before. In sum, if you discover that your employee does not believe that the probability of receiving the promised reward is high, motivation may be the key performance factor.

3. IS THERE A HIGH PERCEIVED PROBABILITY OF ACHIEVING THE LEVEL OF PERFORMANCE NECESSARY TO RECEIVE THE REWARD?

This question speaks to the standard of performance that is needed to receive the reward and the employee's perception as to whether he or she can achieve that level of performance. If the employee believes that he or she probably cannot achieve the level of performance needed to receive the reward (that the standard is set too high), he or she may not be motivated to engage in the given task. Note also that if the standard set for receiving the reward is too low, employees may be motivated only to *meet* that standard rather than to exceed that standard. So if performance is less than exemplary, consider the possibility that the level of performance required for receiving that reward is either too high or too low to motivate exemplary performance. If this turns out to be the case, you can adjust the goals and targets to a lower or higher standard, as appropriate.

A story illustrates what happens when a standard is set too high.

> *A leader at a bank once held a sales contest for the tellers to see who could refer the most people to the new-accounts representative to open a new account or an additional account. To be eligible to receive the prize of a $100 gift certificate to a high-end restaurant, a teller had to refer at least fifty customers to the new-accounts representative in a week. After the fiftieth referral, the teller would receive a ticket for each person he or she referred, and the ticket would be put in a hat for a drawing at the end of the week. The leader thought this standard of fifty referrals was reasonable because one of the tellers had referred fifty-two people during a previous week, thus showing that it could be done. However, although the tellers thought the reward was valuable and sufficient and knew that they would get a ticket for each person they referred over fifty, they all felt that fifty refer-*

*rals was too much of a stretch for them to realistically accom-
plish. On their best week over the past eight months, they had
averaged only twenty-five referrals per teller. And the teller who
had made the fifty-two referrals in one week was working the
lobby and was able to talk with customers as they entered the
line. Because most of the tellers felt that they couldn't get fifty
referrals in a week and therefore would not get even one ticket,
they didn't even try to get referrals. In fact, the only referrals they
made that week were from customers who asked them about
different types of accounts they offered. The average number of
referrals that week was a dismal twenty-two.*

Is the Motivation Factor Key to an Exemplary Strength?

As noted in previous chapters, the process for determining the key performance factor driving the exemplary strength consists of the following steps:

- Scan the performance factors in the model to see if one factor
  for the given task stands out to both you and the employee as
  occurring to a greater degree or in a different form for the employee than for nonexemplary performers.

- If more than one factor is detected, work with the employee to
  narrow the probable factors to the one factor believed to be
  most responsible for exemplary performance.

In support of this process, feel free to look at the diagnostic questions
used to identify the key factor for the expandable strength, making appropriate modifications. Instead of asking the questions as they stand
in the previous section on expandable strengths, you can modify them
to get at the difference between the employee and others who are not
performing the given task at the exemplary level, by asking the following questions:

1. Are the rewards for completing a given task valued more by
   the employee or considered to be more sufficient by the employee than by nonexemplary performers?

2. Does the employee feel that there is a higher probability of receiving the rewards for completing a given task than do other employees?

3. Does the employee feel that there is a higher probability of achieving the level of performance necessary to receive the rewards than do other employees?

An answer of yes to any of the above questions may indicate that the motivation factor is the key performance factor driving exemplary performance. To repeat, though, these questions are not meant to provide the definitive answer on the issue; instead, they are meant to offer helpful information in the larger discussion and assessment that you and the employee will be conducting together during step 2 of the process.

Tools to Develop an Expandable Strength

If you have identified that motivation is the primary performance factor underlying an expandable strength for a given employee, there are a number of tools you can turn to for increasing motivation:

- Tangible rewards (e.g., pay, benefits, contest rewards)
- Intangible rewards (e.g., empowerment, praise, challenging assignments)
- Reinforcement survey
- Goal setting

Which tool or tools you select, of course, depends on whether an employee has expressed dissatisfaction with tangible or intangible rewards and which specific kinds of tangible or intangible rewards the employee has indicated (or you suspect based on observation) will help him or her get excited about accomplishing the work. But you need to do more than narrow down which type of reward to offer (for example, pay versus praise); you also need to flesh out the specifics and make that reward motivating for the employee (e.g., how much of a pay increase? what kind of praise, public or private?).

Your goal is to determine the precise reward that needs to be offered to help motivate an employee to engage in the targeted task. For

---

WHICH REWARDS ARE MORE MOTIVATING: TANGIBLE OR INTANGIBLE?

Intangible rewards tend to be more motivating to people than tangible rewards. In the best-selling book *True North: Discover Your Authentic Leadership*, authors Bill George and Peter Sims indicate that the most effective leaders are motivated by intrinsic needs and rewards.[3] In addition, Edward Deci and Richard Ryan cite research that demonstrates intrinsic motivation has been associated with greater creativity, flexibility, and spontaneity.[4] This research is welcome news for those leaders who do not have the power or flexibility to increase tangible rewards like pay and prizes, as they can turn to less resource-intensive intangible rewards as motivators for exemplary performance. Note that although I present tangible rewards first for ease of communication, intangible rewards tend to be more motivating than tangible rewards.

---

example, do you need to give an employee a pay raise of $5,000 or $25,000 to motivate him to accomplish his work? Would the employee enjoy an extra vacation day or a gift certificate to a local restaurant? Deciding which tool or tools are right for a given employee will involve assessing that person's interests, preferences, and needs.

TANGIBLE REWARDS

As discussed earlier, tangible rewards refers to material things. These include fundamentals such as salary and benefits (e.g., health insurance, life insurance, tuition reimbursement, and employee assistance programs). Salary and benefits may be necessary to motivate employees but not sufficient to do so. Other tangible rewards (those that might be considered supplemental rather than fundamental) include items such as tickets to a movie, a $50 gift certificate to a restaurant, a bonus or pay raise, or an iPod. Part of the challenge is to find an item that is valued and sufficient, which may require some probing. For example, you can ask your employees whether they like to go to the movies or prefer to go to a baseball game. Do they like to go out to dinner? If so, what kind of restaurant would they like to go to for dinner? Do they even like to dine out? Questions like these will help you examine the supplemental tangible rewards you currently give or are planning to give.

In step 2 of the Exemplary Performance Model, you ask about whether motivation is a factor for an expandable strength. If you discover that the tangible reward you are providing for the employee is not working to motivate him or her to engage in the given task, you can have a brainstorming discussion with the employee to determine what the right reward would be. That is, you work together to come up with a reward that will be both valued by and sufficient to the employee, within, of course, the constraints of company resources to supply that reward. If you discover in step 2 that the issue is not the sufficiency or value of the reward but rather doubts that the reward would be delivered as promised or that the employee would be able to do what was necessary to receive the reward, you'll want to look into adjusting the reward system. For example, you might lower the standards to be met to earn the reward or demonstrate a clear commitment to deliver the reward as promised.

INTANGIBLE REWARDS

Intangible rewards, also discussed earlier in the chapter, are abstract rewards you can provide for your employees. They include things like empowerment, praise, challenging assignments, recognition, and appreciation. See table 15 for definitions and examples of intangible rewards.

Other examples of intangible rewards include allowing an employee to work with someone in a job to which he aspires for a half day (reward of development), having a contest in which you wash the car of the winner (reward of appreciation), and reading a customer's compliment to your leader with the employee present (reward of recognition). No matter what type of intangible reward you provide, you will want to examine what the employee would value and consider sufficient. For example, does he like to be recognized in front of his peers or prefer private recognition? Will giving the employee a half-day to work with someone in a job she wants to do in the future be enough time to be rewarding or is an entire day necessary? Will reading a customer's compliment to your leader embarrass the employee or

TABLE 15   **Examples of Intangible Rewards**

REWARD	DEFINITION	EXAMPLE
Empowerment	Providing an opportunity for the employee to make decisions relative to his or her key responsibilities	Allowing an employee to give customers up to a 10% discount without management approval
Praise	Communicating in written or verbal form to the employee your high opinion of his or her work	Telling an employee how well he performed a specific task
Stimulation (or pride) owing to challenging assignments*	Participating in an assignment that is desired by the employee and will help the employee achieve a personal goal such as development of a new skill	Assigning an employee to lead a project team for the first time
Recognition	Acknowledging to one or more people the efforts of the employee to accomplish a task	Mentioning accomplishments of the employee at the team meeting
Appreciation	Thanking the employee for his or her efforts to accomplish the given task	Writing a note to the employee thanking him for working two weekends in a row to meet a deadline
Fulfillment owing to meaningful assignments**	Enabling the employee to work on projects or tasks that match his or her values and sense of what's important	Assigning an employee to lead a recycling program

*Challenging assignments are the tool for delivering the reward of stimulation.
**Meaningful assignments are the tool for delivering the reward of fulfillment.

strengthen his sense of pride in a job well done? Just as with tangible rewards, these types of questions will help you determine intangible rewards that the employee will value and consider sufficient.

REINFORCEMENT SURVEY

A reinforcement survey is a simple survey that asks people to identify the types of rewards they value. The survey is typically structured in one of three ways. The first lists the options available for rewards and has each employee check off the items he or she likes. This method typically focuses on tangible rewards. The second asks open-ended questions to determine the types of rewards each employee would like to receive. This usually yields a list of both tangible and intangible rewards. The third is a hybrid containing both items to check off and open-ended questions. Like the open-ended survey, this hybrid model provides input on both tangible and intangible rewards. Of course, there are other ways to structure your survey, such as having employees rate their desire to receive a particular reward, but in my experience, ratings are used less frequently for reinforcement surveys. You can design the reinforcement survey to assess the sufficiency and value of any and all of the tangible and intangible rewards discussed so far in this chapter.

When in step 2 you were asking the necessary questions to determine whether motivation was the factor most responsible for the employee's exemplary or expandable strengths, you might have discovered that the rewards employees are currently receiving are not valued. A reinforcement survey will help you determine which rewards are valued so that you can change the reward. If you are not at liberty to change the reward, the survey results will at least give you persuasive data to use when discussing the potential rewards system with the person or people who can change the rewards.

Finally, it's easy to forget about fundamentals like pay and benefits when designing a reinforcement survey, but remember that there are times when people are dissatisfied with their pay or benefits package. This may cause them to feel unmotivated, so you will want to inquire about these kind of rewards in your reinforcement surveys. Note also that intangible rewards like satisfaction and pride refer to a personal feeling that is the result of a complex system of decisions and personality variables, so you typically would not ask about these things on a reinforcement survey. They are too difficult to capture in this format.

GOAL SETTING

Goal setting is another tool that will help you develop expandable strengths when motivation is the key factor. In addition to giving employees clear expectations about desired outcomes, an effective goal is, in itself, motivating. To be effective, the goal must be challenging but realistic. This challenge will drive a person to want to achieve something difficult. Achievement is experienced as a reward. A person feels a sense of accomplishment and often receives recognition when challenging goals are achieved or surpassed. The person gets a sense of pride and increased confidence in his or her ability to perform at a higher level. This confidence can cause a virtuous cycle of performance in which a new goal is set with more challenging targets, more achievements, more reinforcement, and even more challenging goals. What is interesting about goal setting is that when goals are challenging and are not achieved, many people want to try harder to accomplish the goal. Rather than being demotivating, a good leader can help the employee see this as a good learning experience and challenge him or her to try again. An abundance of research confirms that goal setting can be an effective performance tool.[5]

Tools to Leverage Motivation

Motivation may be identified as a key enabler of an exemplary strength, but, like talent and fit, motivation itself cannot be transferred from one employee to the next. This is because motivation is a very individual experience. What one person finds motivating, another may not. Nonetheless, a highly motivated employee is in a wonderful position to help others achieve exemplary performance for the given exemplary strength because he or she is engaged in that task and has experience completing it at an extremely high level. As always, the goal is to leverage the targeted exemplary *strength*, not necessarily the *factor* determined to be the key driver of that strength. Because that is the case, you can turn to the tools shown in the model for other factors. In particular, the tools for knowledge and skills—such as training, role modeling, coaching, and stretch assignments—can be implemented in the action plan. Using such tools won't help the employee transfer motivation to other employees, but doing so can certainly help the employee transfer the knowledge and skills needed by employees to complete the given task at the exemplary level. As a result, the employee will be leveraging the exemplary strength to raise the performance of others in the organization.

Who Is Responsible for Addressing Strengths Related to Motivation?

As with the other performance factors, both the leader and the employee are responsible for addressing strengths related to motivation. Both must come together to determine whether or not motivation is the factor that most drives the exemplary and expandable strength because the leader and the employee both have information that contributes to the conversation. For example, you as the leader should share any facts and observations that will help with determining whether or not motivation is the key factor. The employee should share information and participate by self-assessing and sharing perceptions about the level and causes of his or her motivation.

If the motivation factor is determined to be the one most responsible for an exemplary or expandable strength, there are actions that both you and the employee can take. You will capture these in the action plan. For example, both of you should contribute your ideas on how to leverage motivation when it is an exemplary strength or develop it when it's an expandable strength, and both of you should follow through on your action items. Only through a partnership will the most effective action plan be developed.

Using the Model in the Real World

I once had a client named Thomas who was in the financial services industry and who had a particularly challenging employee issue. The person he was working with, Teresa, was a great employee. She had quite a few exemplary strengths and performed at or above standard in every aspect of her job. Teresa had one expandable strength they were struggling with. Teresa was responsible for training salespeople on new banking services, and one of her key responsibilities was designing the training. The expandable skill they chose to examine was researching and learning as much as she could about the new products coming out so that she could design accurate and effective training. After going through the first six factors, they came to the motivation factor. Nothing had emerged in the other factors to indicate that any of them was the key factor underlying Teresa's performance. In answering the diagnostic questions for the motivation factor, Teresa revealed that she didn't see any positive rewards for conducting this research. She understood why she had to do it, but she didn't feel rewarded for doing so.

After uncovering this, the two decided to focus on motivation and determine how she could receive greater rewards given the constraints that they faced. Thomas had no budget to do anything tangible. He also didn't have time to follow up in person each time Teresa conducted this research on a product. However, because she wrote up her findings for use in the training she created, they decided that she would submit those findings to Thomas. He would review the report and would provide feedback. When she did a good job, he would send a note to his boss and let him know that the training was on track due to Teresa's good work.

There were two things that were motivating to Teresa about this plan. First, as Thomas reviewed her reports, she received feedback for her work and was challenged to improve its quality. Second, when she received recognition for her work, she felt a sense of pride—an important intrinsic reward.

Conclusion

At first glance, motivation sometimes appears to be the factor at play for employee performance when it is not. It's easy to assume that if an employee says that he or she feels unmotivated to engage in a task that motivation is the key performance factor. Yet it's important to remember that the larger psychological concept of motivation—the drive to do something—is different from the motivation performance factor itself. The motivation performance factor is more narrowly defined as a person's drive to do something on the basis of the belief that the rewards promised for that work are sufficient and valuable. By using the three diagnostic questions in this chapter, you will be able to differentiate between performance areas where rewards are the key issue (i.e., the key factor is the motivation factor) and performance areas where a problem with one of the other six performance factors is simply leading an employee to feel unmotivated to engage in the targeted task.

Part 3

Applying the Model

10

The Development Process Step by Step

A fter reading chapters 3 through 9 on the performance factors, you are probably starting to get a good handle on how the Exemplary Performance Model actually works. Of course, it's one thing to read about the model and another to use it. So in this chapter I give you guidance to apply the model in the real world. Chapter 2 provided an overview of each of the steps in the model; this chapter will break down each step of the model into the smaller substeps.

A Review of How the Model Works

As described in chapter 2, the following four steps comprise the Exemplary Performance Model:

1. **Assess and target performance**—Identify an employee's strengths and weaknesses and select one exemplary strength (a task that yields exemplary results when engaged in by the employee) and one expandable strength (a task that yields at-standards or greater results but less than exemplary results,

and has the potential to become exemplary) to target; set weaknesses aside.

2. **Diagnose cause(s) of performance**—Determine the cause (key performance factor) yielding the high performance associated with the exemplary strength and the cause (key performance factor) keeping the expandable strength from becoming an exemplary one.

3. **Develop and implement a plan**—Develop an action plan that applies the right tool(s) to leverage the exemplary strength (transfer it to others) and the right tool(s) to develop the expandable strength; then work with the employee to implement the plan.

4. **Follow up**—Follow up to see how the performance development process is working to leverage and develop the targeted strengths, and adjust the action plan if needed.

Each step of the Exemplary Performance Model involves substeps that you will use to apply the model with employees in a hands-on way.

Benchmarking

Before starting through the model, you will first need to do some benchmarking to determine the level of performance that qualifies as exemplary—that is, exactly how "significantly above" standards does performance need to be to be considered exemplary? Ideally, you will select the benchmark for exemplary results from exemplars *in the industry* rather than exemplars in your organization. For example, if you are examining a recruiter's task of sourcing quality candidates, as measured by the candidates' turnover within the first year of employment, you would want to compare the results that the recruiter produces when engaging in that task with the results attained by the recruiting exemplar in the recruiting industry. Through professional associations and Web sites in this industry, such as the Society for Human Resource Management (SHRM) and HR.com, you can determine the top performers in recruiting and use their performance as the benchmark. Note that when measures for exemplary performance are not available, you and your employee should work to come to agreement on whether to label a strength as exemplary or expandable. If

you do not agree, you can keep the task in the general strengths category until a future time and revisit the issue for development once you have additional behavioral or outcome data to guide you in how the strength should be labeled.

It's important to benchmark against exemplars in the industry in order to expand your view of what is possible. A lim-

Ideally, you will select the benchmark for exemplary results from exemplars **in the industry** *rather than exemplars in your organization so you are developing performance to the highest level of attainable performance.*

ited view may cause us to believe that the person at our organization who performs a particular task the best represents the highest attainable level of performance. By benchmarking performance at the industry level, we might discover that there is a much higher level of performance that can be attained.

Step 1: Assess and Target Performance

Now let's examine the substeps of assessing and targeting performance (step 1).

The goal of step 1 is to identify an employee's strengths and decide which two strengths are the most important and impactful strengths to target at this time. There are three basic substeps that will help you fulfill this goal, as shown in the following box.

STEP 1: ASSESS AND TARGET PERFORMANCE

A. Identify employee strengths and weaknesses; set the weaknesses aside.

B. Separate the employee's strengths into exemplary strengths and expandable strengths

C. Select one exemplary strength and one expandable strength to target.

STEP 1A: IDENTIFY THE EMPLOYEE'S STRENGTHS AND WEAKNESSES

To assess an employee's strengths and weaknesses, you will need to have a copy of the employee's job profile in front of you. As noted in chapter 2, an effective job profile will contain a list of the tasks, key responsibilities, knowledge, skills, abilities, and behaviors required for success in a given job, as well as the level of performance (in terms of standards and metrics) required for the job. If you do not currently have this information for a given position, it is essential that you generate it before using the Exemplary Performance Model. With the job profile in hand, you and the employee will examine each of the profile's tasks and assess which of them represent strengths and which represent weaknesses for the employee. Remember, strengths represent those tasks that yield at-standards or above results, with potential for improvement (if not already at the exemplary level); weaknesses represent those tasks that yield at-standards or below results, with little or no potential for improvement. Tasks that the employee is currently performing below standards with room for improvement should also be categorized as weaknesses for purposes of using this model. Set the weaknesses aside.

STEP 1B: SEPARATE EMPLOYEE STRENGTHS INTO EXEMPLARY STRENGTHS AND EXPANDABLE STRENGTHS

Once you have sorted the employee's tasks into strengths and weaknesses, you are ready to categorize the strengths as exemplary or expandable. (Note: If any of the weaknesses occur in critical areas of an employee's job, these should be earmarked to be addressed in the performance management process rather than in the performance development process. The present model can be used to develop weaknesses in the performance management process; however, in the performance development process, the focus should be on leveraging and developing strengths.) To make this categorization, you and the employee will identify which strengths are already yielding exemplary results (exemplary strengths) and which strengths have the potential to yield exemplary results (expandable strengths). Note that an employee may not have any exemplary strengths at this time. If she does not, you don't want her to feel demotivated or demoralized. Let her

SHOULD THE RESULTS FOR EVERY TASK BE MEASURED?

Whether you are assessing current employee results or simply setting benchmarks, measuring results for some tasks, as in the case of tasks related to soft skills such as giving quality feedback or communicating effectively, can be difficult. Or it may simply be more effort than it's worth to make such measurements. For example, if you want to determine whether an administrative assistant is producing exemplary results or at-standards results or better for the task of greeting individuals as they enter the department, do you really have the time or interest in assessing those results by, say, counting the number of individuals the administrative assistant greets each day or gathering assessments of her level of friendliness? Probably not. Instead, you and the employee can enter into a conversation in which you discuss the observable behaviors and measurable outcomes that reveal the employee's level of performance in greeting individuals. For example, you may observe a small sample of the assistant's greetings, discuss the behaviors and outcomes of exemplar greeters, and ask the assistant if she thinks that her behaviors and outcomes match those of the exemplar. If you and she both assess that she is at the level of performance of the exemplary standard, then this is an exemplary strength. If you and she both assess that she is not at the exemplary standard but that with some help she can get there, then this is an expandable strength.

know that development is a process, not an event. It takes time to achieve exemplary status. Not having an exemplary strength doesn't mean the employee lacks the potential to be exemplary, just that she is not there yet. Remind her that it is common when first using the model not to find any exemplary strengths and that by using the model now and in the future, she will begin building her list of exemplary strengths over time.

The first time you sit down to engage in step 1 of the model with an employee, you will spend a good deal of time examining each task and labeling it as a weakness, an exemplary strength, or an expandable strength, given that there are many tasks for any given job. However, once you put forth this initial effort, you will have a substantial list of the employee's strengths to return to time and time again as you repeat the performance development cycle and return to step 1. Thus, step 1 will take less time to complete in future development cycles.

If you'd like to use a shortcut in the process, you can begin step 1 by assessing the *key responsibilities* that overarch employee tasks (rather than starting at the task level) and labeling these as weaknesses or strengths. You can then zero in on one key responsibility that is a strength and its requisite set of tasks, and work with only this set of tasks in the next few cycles of performance development. Of course, you will want to pick a key responsibility that is important and impactful for this approach to be worthwhile. (See the next section for insight into how to make this judgment.)

STEP 1C: SELECT ONE EXEMPLARY STRENGTH AND ONE EXPANDABLE STRENGTH TO TARGET

Once a list of exemplary and expandable strengths has been created, you and your employee are ready to select one of each kind of strength to target in this first cycle of performance development.

The criteria for selecting a strength to leverage or develop are the following:

1. Is the given strength (task) important to the department's or organization's goals?

2. Will the given strength (task) produce the desired outcomes if targeted?

Importance

To determine the importance of the task that correlates with a particular strength, look at whether or not the desired outcomes of the task directly support the achievement of a departmental or organizational goal. If the key responsibility under which that task falls directly maps to a departmental or organizational goal (i.e., is a direct driver of that goal rather than being an enabler of that goal), it falls into the *important* category and may be worth addressing. For example, closing new business is a key responsibility that will *directly drive* the department's sales goal. In contrast, the task of calling sales prospects each day will help drive the sales goal but probably does not tie directly to the department's goal. It simply *enables* the accomplishment of the sales goal.

Naturally, any key responsibility that directly drives revenue goals is considered to be of high importance and is desirable for targeting if potential for significant impact is also found to exist.

Impact

To determine whether the impact of addressing a given strength (task) is sufficient, you will want to spend some time assessing the impact that leveraging or developing this strength is expected to have on the department's or team's strategic goals. In other words, how much return on expectations (ROE; i.e., the benefit expected given the work you will have to do) is anticipated? Does the ROE outweigh the time and energy invested in the leveraging or developing process? Answering these questions will provide more insight into choosing which strengths to target.

For example, if an employee spends time leveraging his exemplary strength of creating well-designed desktop publishing documents but the rest of the employees in the department lack talent in this task and aren't expected to improve much through the leveraging process, it is unlikely that leveraging this strength will have much impact (low ROE) on key departmental goals, so it's preferable not to target this strength. Similarly, if the employee spends time developing his expandable strength of cross-departmental collaboration but is expected to work only individually or with others on his team after developing this strength, the impact of developing this strength wouldn't be that great (low ROE) and isn't worth targeting. Note that cross-departmental collaboration is *important* in this situation but not *impactful,* so it would not be targeted.

Assessing Importance and Impact Together

Let's look at how you might apply the importance and impact criteria together. Imagine that you've labeled an employee's ability to write effective e-mail responses to customer inquiries as an expandable strength. Yet when deciding whether to target this expandable strength, you realize that this task is not terribly important to the person's job, as he does not perform it very often. If you try to develop that strength, improvements will not yield measurable results that have an impact on the department's goals. So you decide not to target it during the devopment process. Or say you look at the employee's

FIGURE 7 **The Exemplary Performance Model Process**

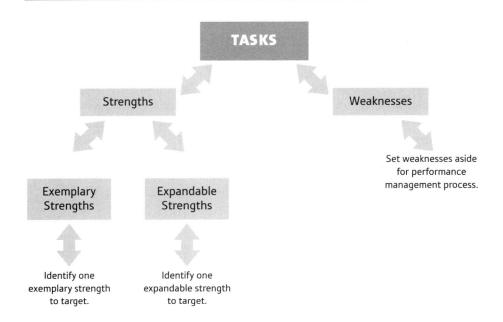

expandable strength of effectively addressing in-person customer complaints. You see that this task is critically important to the employee's job, and it is also important to the department's ability to achieve its goals (it has high ROE through better customer retention). Because addressing in-person complaints is both important and impactful, you choose to target this particular expandable strength.

As can be seen in figure 7, you will end up with four "buckets" of tasks. First you divide the key responsibilities and tasks into two buckets, one for strengths and one for weaknesses. Then you divide the strengths into two buckets, one for an exemplary strength and one for an expandable strength to diagnose in step 2.

I'm often asked what to do about weaknesses. Although the focus of this book and the model is to develop exemplary performance, weaknesses may be improved through use of the model. The determining factor will be the employee's talent for the task and potential to improve. Because performance development is a continuous process, addressing expandable strengths may cause performance of weaknesses to improve even though they are not the focus. For example, I conduct many presentations. If I have an expandable strength in preparing for presentations and improve performance in that area, weaknesses in other tasks (such as displaying a strong presence when starting a presentation) may improve as a result of being better prepared. Also, if a weakness is not in a key area of performance, it is not fruitful to focus on it.

Ultimately, don't worry about selecting the absolute "best" exemplary strength and expandable strength to target. As long as your own and your employee's assessment of the task as a strength is accurate and the task has some degree of importance and expected impact, it will pay to work on that area. If you later discover that a different strength has greater importance or impact, you can focus on that strength in the future. Remember that the development process is not a finite process with a single completion date but instead is a cycle that will be repeated continually.

Step 2: Diagnose Cause(s) of Performance

The goal of step 2 is to figure out the key factors underlying the targeted performance areas so you can capitalize on that knowledge and create an effective performance action plan in step 3. In step 2 you will focus on identifying which performance factor is most responsible for the employee's ability to perform at an exemplary level for the targeted exemplary strength and which performance factor most explains the gap between the current performance level and the exemplary level for the expandable strength. The substeps involved in this process are shown in the box on the following page.

As reflected in the box on the next page and as evidenced in all of the chapters on performance factors (chapters 3–9), the process for diagnosing the cause of the exemplary strength varies somewhat from that of diagnosing the cause of the expandable strength.

The goal when diagnosing the cause of the exemplary strength is to identify the particular factor that most represents the difference between the exemplary performance of the employee for the given strength compared with those performing at a level that is less than ex-

STEP 2: DIAGNOSING CAUSE(S) OF PERFORMANCE

A. Identify which performance factor is most responsible for the exemplary strength.

- Scan the performance factors to see whether you and the employee can identify one factor that occurs to a greater degree or in a different form for the employee than for nonexemplary performers for the given task.

- If more than one factor is detected, work with the employee to narrow the probable factors to the one factor believed to be most responsible for exemplary performance.

B. Identify the factor with the highest potential to increase the expandable strength to the exemplary level.

- Review each factor, asking whether or not this factor is the most significant reason for the task being an expandable strength.

- Narrow the probable factors to the most influential factor.

emplary. You can safely assume that most, if not all, of the performance factors are present in the case of exemplary performance, so you are not looking for the *presence* of factors so much as you are trying to determine which of the present factors highlights a *difference* between the exemplary employee and others.

The goal when diagnosing the cause of the expandable strength is to identify the particular factor that best explains the gap between the current level of performance and exemplary performance. Unlike for the exemplary strength, you can't assume that all of the factors are present when diagnosing the factor for the expandable strength. In fact, often the *lack* of a particular factor is what's responsible for the current level of "expandable" performance. Or the performance factor for the expandable strength might be present for the employee but in a problematic form. So the process of diagnosing the key performance factor for the expandable strength will involve examining each of the factors in the model to detect which one or ones might not be present or might be present in a problematic form. If more than one factor is identified as lacking or problematic, you and the employee will work together to narrow down this list of factors to the one factor believed to most explain the difference between the employee's performance for a given task and exemplary performance. That is, which factor is most holding the employee back from achieving exemplary performance? If you worry about picking the "best" factor, just keep in mind that this is a process and not an event. You may come back at a later time to address other factors that may be the reason for performance not yet reaching the exemplary level.

EXEMPLARY STRENGTH

To identify which performance factor is most responsible for the exemplary strength, you and the employee will review the performance factors in the model and have a conversation to pinpoint which factor or factors seem to differentiate the employee from nonexemplary performers for the given task. You will base this discussion on your observations, assessment, and measures of the employee's performance as well as on the employee's own self-assessment. If you need additional support and guidance in this part of the process, you can use the diagnostic questions described in each of the chapters on performance factors (chapters 3–9) for the exemplary strength (see also appendix B).

If you and the employee identify more than one possible key factor, your goal should be to work together until you can come to agreement on which factor to target. Selecting one particular factor doesn't mean that the other factor or factors lack value or relevance; instead, doing so keeps the development process focused, efficient, and manageable. If necessary, you can return to the other factor or factors that don't get selected in future cycles of the performance development process.

Because the selection of the key performance factor involves a subjective process of observation and self-assessment, you may choose to do some research during step 3 of the process (develop an action plan) to make sure you've identified the right factor before taking the time and effort to use a given tool to leverage the targeted strength. In some cases, the time and effort of doing research will be worthwhile; in other cases, the returns on your time and effort probably won't be worth it.

For example, if you plan to invest thousands of dollars to roll out training that is based on the assumption that you've identified the right factor for an employee's exemplary strength, it will be worth your time to do some research first (e.g., determine whether the training will address a lack of exemplary performance in others or determine the value of expected performance improvements). Your research might save you thousands of dollars on ineffective or unnecessary training.

In contrast, if you are simply going to have an employee make a presentation at a monthly team meeting of some new knowledge he learned at a conference, knowledge that helps him to accomplish the exemplary task, then you may not find it worth your time to do any research to confirm whether you've selected the absolute most relevant performance factor. Because the employee's presentation does not cost thousands of dollars to deliver or take employees away from their regular duties, there's no great risk to the employee making this presentation.

EXPANDABLE STRENGTH

To identify the factor with the highest potential to increase the expandable strength to the exemplary level, you can begin by asking the three diagnostic questions for each factor, as described in chapters 3–9 and summarized in appendix B. These questions, having not been tested for scientific reliability and validity at the time of this book's publication, are not intended to serve as stand-alone indicators of whether a given performance factor is at play, but they can nonetheless serve as useful aids for zeroing in on the key performance factor when used in conjunction with the overall assessments and judgments of you and your employee.

If, during the process of identifying the key factor for the expandable strength, you narrow down the list of possible factors somewhat but still need to select only one (the *key* performance factor) to address, I recommend that you focus on determining which one factor accounts for the *greatest percentage* of performance relative to that task. Note that this assessment will be determined through discussions with your employee, by gathering relevant measures of performance, and by documenting observations of performance when available. Once you select the one factor that you both believe is the key performance factor, don't fret about whether you've made the right selection. As long as you have some evidence (observations, measures) that the factor is affecting performance, addressing it will be useful when developing the targeted strength.

Step 3: Develop and Implement a Plan

Once you have determined the key performance factor for each of the targeted strengths (exemplary and expandable), you can move on to creating a customized action plan in order to leverage and develop the targeted strengths. The goal of the action plan for leveraging the exemplary strength is to create the most effective plan possible for sharing the strength with others. The goal of the action plan for developing the expandable strength is to create the most effective plan possible to help the employee raise performance to the exemplary level.

The substeps of this process are shown in the following box.

STEP 3: DEVELOP AND IMPLEMENT A PLAN

A. Select the appropriate tools.

B. Create goals to put the tools into action.

C. Schedule a follow-up date.

STEP 3A: SELECT THE APPROPRIATE TOOLS

In step 3, you begin by identifying which tool or tools you and the employee anticipate will work best to help you leverage or develop the targeted strength. The outer ring of the model provides a number of potential tools, which are discussed in chapters 3–9, and you will typically want to zero in on the tools associated with the selected underlying factor when developing the action plan. If none of these tools seem quite right, you and the employee can brainstorm about possible tools not listed in the model, or even turn to the model for tools listed for a factor other than the one selected.

For example, the reason for a particular exemplary strength might be that the individual has a specific process he or she goes through for a given task. For a construction superintendent, it might be the process she goes through to ensure subcontractors arrive at the job site at the exact time expected. Naturally, the systems and processes factor would be the reason for the exemplary strength. However, creating an action plan to share her knowledge of the new process through *informal training and demonstration* might be the best tool to use to leverage this strength. This tool is associated with the knowledge and skills factor in the model, not the systems and processes factor. The tools grouped by factor in the model are intended to be helpful in choosing the right tool, but there is no need to feel limited to using only those tools shown for a given factor.

STEP 3B: CREATE GOALS TO PUT THE TOOLS INTO ACTION

Once you've identified the tools you will be incorporating into the action plan, you will focus on setting goals for putting those tools into action. When setting goals, you want to do the following:

- Create specific and measurable goals.
- Determine actions, responsibilities, and timelines.

Create Specific and Measurable Goals

In creating goals, first capture specifically what you will do during step 3 (action planning) and how that will be measured. The first part of goal setting is being specific. Vague or general statements will not help you determine what you and the employee need to do. The more specific you are in terms of how you will use the tool to address the strength, the more the goal will be able to drive your actions. For example, if the tool you will use is to create a job aid, a template to document patient charges more accurately (tools and resources), your action plan should be specific and state that the goal is to "create a template containing fields for all relevant patient billing information by the end of the month." This is a stronger goal than "create a billing template."

The second part of goal setting is ensuring measurement. Measurement is critical to gauging success and determining whether or not the goal needs to be adjusted. You will not be able to determine whether the goal is *accomplished* and the employee is successful unless the goal can be measured. For example, the goal to create a template for billing information contains two measures: (1) a quality check of the template to ensure it contains all the relevant information needed to bill patients, and (2) a timeline to have the template completed by the end of the month.

Determine Actions, Responsibilities, and Timelines

To successfully complete each of the goals, you will need to determine what actions are required, who is responsible for each action, and when each action needs to be completed. This information is useful for a number of reasons. First, it will make clear who will do what by when in working toward accomplishing the goal, and, second, the information will be critical for enabling you to give meaningful feedback in step 4 (follow-up). That is, when you meet with the employee to follow up on his or her action plan, you will work together to determine the status of each action step for each goal (e.g., Has progress been made? Has the action been completed? Are there other roadblocks that prevent an action from being completed? Is the step still relevant?).

STEP 3C: SCHEDULE A FOLLOW-UP DATE

The last substep of step 3 is to set a date to meet for follow-up (in preparation for step 4). The date selected will be determined on a case-by-case basis. You can use your goals and action plans as a source of information that will help you determine how frequently to meet. Longer-term goals may require more time between meetings. However, you don't want your first follow-up meeting to be scheduled on the due date of the goal, as this will not allow you to take corrective measures to get back on track if the action plan is not working. Overall, you can use your best judgment to determine the frequency of follow-up.

Step 4: Follow Up

At the follow-up stage, you will be checking in with the employee to discuss the progress you and the employee have made toward completing the action plan. There are two goals for this step. First, you want to recognize and reinforce the employee's progress. Whether focusing on an exemplary or expandable strength, the employee will most likely have made progress toward his or her goals, and this is an opportunity to recognize recent successes and improvements. In the case of an exemplary strength, you might recognize the improvements *in others* that are a direct result of leveraging the particular strength. In the case of an expandable strength, you might recognize the individual's own progress and performance improvement. Second, if the desired results are not being achieved, you can collaborate to make changes to the action plan and get back on track. The substeps of this step are shown in the following box.

STEP 4: FOLLOW UP

A. Review the status of the action plan for the exemplary strength.

B. Start the process again for a new exemplary strength, if appropriate.

C. Review the status of the action plan for the expandable strength.

D. Start the process again for a new expandable strength, if appropriate.

When reviewing the action plan for each strength, you will ask the employee to describe the progress he or she has made on each of the action items, and you will share your own progress as well, if applicable. You will also provide information and measures as to what you have observed in terms of the performance in others in the case of an exemplary strength or in terms of the employee's own performance in the case of an expandable strength. Similarly, the employee should share information and measures that he or she has gathered relative to each goal. If the employee has encountered challenges to completing the action plan, you will make adjustments to accommodate these challenges at the follow-up stage so he or she can complete the action plan. For example, if you discover that the employee needs more budget to purchase a piece of equipment, you can make changes to the action plan to include you securing or approving additional budget. If you discover that the tools you've selected aren't working effectively (e.g., changing the cubicle the employee sits in has not improved performance on the expandable strength of improving the quality of customer interactions), you will want to adjust the action plan to include new tools (e.g., purchase of a headset for the phone so that the employee can talk and type at the same time).

If you discover at follow-up that the employee has completed the action plan, you will return to step 1 of the model. At this point, you may choose to target the same strength again (if you assess that there is more capacity to share with others for the exemplary strength or still room for growth for the expandable strength) or you may decide to move on and target a new strength. Note that you may decide to target a new strength even if capacity to leverage or develop the previously targeted strength still exists. You may move on because you are satisfied with the current degree of leveraging or developing and prefer to move on to leveraging or developing a new strength. And you may come back to targeting the same strength at another time, especially if you want it to become exemplary as I recommend (for expandable strengths) or if you want to get other employees to the exemplary level through leveraging this strength (for exemplary strengths). There is no dictate that says you have to achieve exemplary performance in one turn of this model's cycle. The exemplary standard is a high one, so it can (and probably will) take multiple cycles, not necessarily engaged in consecutively, to achieve exemplary performance.

Overview of the Steps

So there you have it—a hands-on description of how to apply the model in the real world with each of your employees. Table 16 provides a summary of which questions are being asked and answered at each stage of the development process, along with a list of the deliverables you can expect to create while working through the development process.

TABLE 16 **Questions Asked at Each Step of the Model**

STEP	QUESTION	DELIVERABLE
Create a detailed job profile (prerequisite).	• What are the key responsibilities, tasks, knowledge, skills, abilities, behaviors, standards, and metrics that must be met for success in a given job? • What are the desired measurable outcomes for this job and the organizational goals these outcomes map to?	• A list of key responsibilities, tasks, knowledge, skills abilities, behaviors, standards, and metrics required of employees in a given job • A list of desired, measurable outcomes, which align with organizational goals
1. Assess and target performance.	• How is the employee performing on each of the tasks in which he is engaging (strengths versus weaknesses)? Which strengths are exemplary and which are expandable? • Which one exemplary and one expandable strength should you target at this time?	• A comprehensive list of the tasks that the employee is performing at the exemplary level, the tasks he is performing well but has room to improve on, and the tasks he or she has little potential to improve on • An exemplary strength (if one exists) and an expandable strength to target (two strengths that are impactful and important)

Other Considerations When Applying the Model

When applying the model, you will want to keep several things in mind. These considerations are important regardless of the step on which you are engaged.

ROLE OF SELF-ASSESSMENT: A COLLABORATIVE PROCESS

As discussed in chapter 2, the Exemplary Performance Model involves a collaborative process between you and your employees. That

TABLE 16 CONT'D

STEP	QUESTION	DELIVERABLE
2. Diagnose cause(s) of performance.	• What primary performance factor drives the exemplary strength or explains the gap between current and exemplary performance in the expandable strength?	• The respective factors that most account for the exemplary strength and the expandable strength (one factor for each)
3. Develop and implement a plan.	• Which tools will help you and the employee leverage the exemplary strength and develop the expandable strength? • What goals and actions will support use of the selected tool to leverage the exemplary strength and develop the expandable strength?	• For each type of strength, a list of goals for using each tool, complete with an action plan for each goal
4. Follow up.	• How is the action plan working? • What progress have you and the employee made? • What should happen next given the degree of progress to date?	• Progress update of work toward the action plan for each strength • Recognition for progress and contribution • Next steps for using the model

is why I always mention that both you and your employee will be participating when I offer guidelines for engaging in each step of the process. Whether you are categorizing tasks as strengths and weaknesses, identifying which strengths to target at a given time, searching for the key performance factors underlying the targeted strengths, or creating an action plan to leverage and develop strengths, you and your employees will work together to generate answers. Not only will you be soliciting input from your employees, but you will also be actively engaged in offering your employees support by taking on action items that will help leverage or develop employee performance, as appropriate, and by mentoring your employees throughout the development process.

You gain many benefits by engaging in a collaborative performance development process. First, by actively involving your employees in the development process (rather than dictating to your employees), you gain commitment (rather than mere compliance). Second, by capitalizing on the advantages that both you and the employees uniquely bring to the table—your own power as a leader to effect change in realms beyond the employees' control and the employees' valuable insight into their performance and the factors driving that performance—you increase the effectiveness of the development process. Third, by collaborating with employees, you are helping them gain the ability to self-assess. Since you can't always be present with your employees, the skill of being able to accurately self-assess will help employees reflect on each performance immediately upon completion and determine what went well and how they can improve. Outstanding performers are constantly using the information they have on past performance to improve.

Regardless of which step of the model you are conducting, you and your employees will work together to generate answers.

DEALING WITH THE EXEMPLARY AND EXPANDABLE STRENGTHS IN TANDEM

Although during the first cycle of the development process you will likely be moving through steps 1–4 simultaneously for the exemplary and the expandable strengths, you may get out of sync once you start to repeat the cycle. For example, you and the employee may finish the action plan items for leveraging the exemplary strength before you complete those for developing the expandable strength. If this is the case, you will return to step 1 for the exemplary strength while remaining in step 4 (follow up) for the expandable strength. Because the employee may leverage and develop strengths at a different pace, you and the employee may be engaging in two different steps of the process at any given time—one for the exemplary strength and one for the expandable strength.

Although the model guides you to engage in step 1 for both the exemplary and the expandable strength, then move on to step 2 for each, and finally to steps 3 and 4, you may have wondered, is it okay to engage in steps 1–4 for the exemplary strength and then go back and engage in steps 1–4 for the expandable strength? As long as both types of strengths are addressed (when exemplary strengths are present) and steps 1–4 are covered in order, this is largely a matter of preference.

DOCUMENTING DEVELOPMENT DISCUSSIONS

How you document your development discussions is also a matter of preference; what's most important is that you select a method with which you and the employee both feel comfortable, that the process is consistent, and that you do indeed keep some kind of documentation. Documentation is useful because it captures details of the development conversation so that you don't have to rely on memory, helps to ensure there is a clear understanding of what was covered, and, in some cases, provides information for the performance management process.

Here are some possible methods for documenting your development discussions:

- Create a template to be used to document each discussion, and complete it with the employee at each meeting. This may help guide the discussion as well as document it.
- Designate the written action plan for each targeted strength as your documentation and attach progress notes to the action plan after each follow-up meeting.
- Send a thank-you note to the employee detailing the discussion (i.e., thanking the employee for his or her participation and recognizing progress), and keep a copy for your records.

These are just a few ideas on how to document the development process. If none of these appeal to you, you might develop some other form of documentation to capture what is happening during the process. Just make sure the method is consistent and clear and covers the following essential elements:

- The list of exemplary strengths, expandable strengths, and weaknesses

- The strengths currently being targeted
- The action plan to leverage or develop each strength
- Progress notes from follow-up meetings

Finally, note that although I often refer to action plan in the singular, as if there is only one, you will actually want to create two action plans—one for the exemplary strength and one for the expandable strength (each in a separate document)—because the employee may complete the action plan for one before completing the other. By documenting exemplary and expandable to-do items in separate documents, you will find it easier to file one action plan away after it has been completed while keeping the other action plan active until it is finished.

Conclusion

I hope that after reading this chapter you have the foundational guidance you need to start using the Exemplary Performance Model with your employees. If you ever find yourself feeling overwhelmed, just remember that it's okay to take your time with the model and that each time you use it, you will likely become more comfortable using it to leverage and develop employee performance. Similarly, the steps and factors will likely become ingrained in your employees' minds, such that they may find themselves using them in impromptu settings outside of development meetings to continually tweak and fine-tune their performance. Therein lies one of the great benefits of the model: by involving employees in a collaborative process of performance development, you train them to use the model independently every day. As a result, exemplary performance becomes the norm, not the anomaly, in your workplace.

Rolling Out the Model in the Real World

The steps of the Exemplary Performance Model are simple and straightforward:

1. Assess current performance and target one exemplary strength and one expandable strength.

2. Determine the key factors.

3. Create an action plan to leverage and develop the exemplary and expandable strengths.

4. Follow up.

My aim has always been to provide a clear, straightforward means for leaders to help employees develop to the exemplary level. A leader shouldn't need a specialization in the field of HR, learning, or organization development to develop employees, and this model does not by any means require such a specialization.

Nonetheless, in the real world there are certain challenges to any method of developing performance.

Challenges

The challenges you might encounter while engaging in the Exemplary Performance Model include:

- Driving the process without buy-in from leadership
- Driving performance in a way that aligns with strategy
- Committing to the performance development process and staying motivated
- Adopting the right leadership style
- Avoiding pitfalls during the four steps of the process

DRIVING THE PROCESS WITHOUT BUY-IN FROM LEADERSHIP

In all of my experience using the Exemplary Performance Model, I have found the majority of organizations to be excited about the opportunity to develop their employees to the exemplary level. Yet within any particular organization, top leadership may not buy in to the value of performance development. If your leadership does not buy in to the use of a performance development model in the workplace, you will be faced with a difficult predicament: to use the model without buy-in or to abandon the model altogether. Without buy-in, you might face the following limitations:

- You might have only limited time to spend on performance development.
- You might have limited access to resources (training, equipment, funding, etc.) for developing performance.
- Employees are likely to receive signals from leadership that performance development is not a priority, which can be demotivating.

Each of these limitations has the potential to diminish your ability to use the model successfully. For the model to work in an optimal and maximal way, you really do want to obtain buy-in from your leadership, and I encourage you to do everything you can to obtain that buy-in.

That being said, I am an eternal optimist. So I present the following creative solutions to using the model in spite of a lack of buy-in from top leadership:[1]

- Be creative about freeing up time to focus on performance development.

- Take stock of available resources (rather than focusing on what you don't have).

- Continually communicate benefits and performance improvements to generate excitement and possibly change the mind of your leader.

Finding Time

If you don't have official support for conducting performance development, you will need to be creative about finding time to squeeze in performance development. One way to do this is to free up some time by delegating a few tasks (for both yourself and the employee, if possible) to others. In addition, you might be able to fit in performance development efforts at a monthly lunch meeting or by staying a few minutes later than normal. Another option would be to conduct performance development virtually, by e-mail. You and employees can then exchange ideas when it's most convenient to each of you. Finally, to make efficient use of your time, you can also use abbreviated versions of the tools suggested. For example, instead of sending someone to a full-day training class, you can encourage her to read a book, do some Internet research, or engage in more efficient computer-based training to augment skills or knowledge. Or instead of engaging in formal process mapping, you can map process yourself, quickly and informally.

Finding Resources

Without top leadership buy-in, you might also have less access to resources. I like to remind leaders to be thorough about taking stock of current resources instead of always assuming they need to ask for something new or additional. For example, consider the following:

- Seeking free resources from the Internet (training classes, best practices, data)

- Diverting current training funds to cover other development efforts

- Finding out what resources your employees have and asking them to share

- Talking with your peers at other companies to see if they have resources you can borrow

For other ideas on how to use your current resources creatively, refer to table 8.

Lastly, once employees begin to achieve exemplary performance, you will attain tangible results to share with top leaders. In this way, you may be able to gain buy-in from senior leaders over time. For example, as Juan focused on improving the process for checking the quality of fire alarms his company produced, he was able to check more alarms and catch more defects than before. This improvement caused a drop in the number of "buy-backs" (products the company had to buy back from a retail operation owing to the part being defective), saving the company thousands of dollars. Laurie, his leader, was able to communicate these results to upper management and tie the performance improvement to her use of the model. After learning about the results achieved by the model, management changed their minds about using the model and required all leaders to use it and report results.

DRIVING PERFORMANCE IN A WAY
THAT ALIGNS PERFORMANCE WITH STRATEGY

As discussed in chapter 1, the most important thing you can do for your organization is to drive the execution of strategy. Therefore, in all of your performance development efforts with employees, you want to ensure that the performance you are working to leverage and develop aligns with the larger strategies of your department and your organization. Your guiding goal should always be to develop performance in a direction that aligns with organizational strategy. If you don't align performance development initiatives with organizational strategy, you are doing something like climbing to the top of a ladder that is leaning on the wrong wall. You'll get to the top of the wall, but doing so won't help you achieve desired outcomes.

Ensure that the performance you are working to develop aligns with the larger strategies of your department and your organization.

The best way to ensure that the performance development process stays aligned with organizational strategy is to begin with a job profile that is aligned with organizational strategy. In particular, the key responsibilities, tasks, metrics, and standards (desired out-

TABLE 17 Examples of Tasks Aligned with Organizational Goal

TASK	STANDARDS AND METRICS ALIGNED WITH ORGANIZATIONAL GOAL
Organizational Goal: Rating of 4.5 on industry's 5-point customer service scale	
Answer customers' calls	Answer 95 percent of calls before the third ring
Accurately communicate information	Achieve an average quality score of 4.5 or better
Respond to customers' questions and complaints efficiently	Keep average hold time to less than thirty seconds
Resolve customers' questions or complaints the first time they call	Resolve 90 percent of questions or complaints during the first call

comes) of the job should support the execution of organizational strategy. For example, if your organization's strategy is to be first in customer service, and, as a result, your goal is to achieve a rating of 4.5 on a 5-point scale for the industry's leading customer service index, the key responsibilities, tasks, standards, and metrics in relevant employees' job profiles should support that organizational goal, as reflected in table 17. Because the performance development process for each employee is based on these elements of the job profile, alignment of these elements with organizational goals helps drive the execution of strategy.

By ensuring that an employee's key responsibilities, tasks, standards, and metrics align with organizational strategy, you will also be ensuring that any efforts you and your employees invest in developing their performance on those key responsibilities and tasks will support organizational strategy. In the end, exemplary performance is not just about engaging in tasks at the exemplary level but about engaging in *important and impactful* tasks at the exemplary level. Doing so will help you foster performance that executes organizational strategy.

COMMITTING TO THE PERFORMANCE DEVELOPMENT PROCESS

It's the norm these days for businesses to run at mach speed and for leaders and employees to be in a continual state of intense effort and multitasking. Thus, it's easy to let performance development efforts fall to the bottom of the priority list. Yet there is a great deal to be gained by helping your employees develop their performance—not only in improved efficiency, productivity, and revenues but also in intangibles like high morale and motivation. If you want to effectively develop your employees, you need to commit to the process through self-management. Even if you do have buy-in from top leadership to engage in performance development, at the end of the day it will be up to you to:

- Keep yourself motivated

- Set aside time to develop each of your employees

- Seek out the necessary resources to complete the action plans generated throughout the performance development process

Staying Motivated

If you have not already been engaging in regular performance development efforts with your employees, the idea of finding time to work these efforts into your schedule can be daunting. You will be able to more smoothly make the transition to developing performance on a regular basis if you are willing to see your fundamental role as a leader as one of *developing people*. Although you surely have numerous concrete outcomes that you must deliver to your own leaders day in and day out, the truth is that to be an effective executor of strategy, you need to be supported by a *team* of effective executors of strategy, and the best way to ensure an effective team is to focus on developing it, one employee at a time.

You will be able to make the transition to developing performance on a regular basis if you are willing to see your fundamental role as a leader as one of developing people.

Although performance development may at first seem like a luxury, once you see its positive effects in action, you will discover that it is not a luxury but is instead an essential process—one that allows you to meet deadlines, fulfill departmental and organizational goals, and outstrip your competition. By developing your employees, you will be contributing to your own success as a leader too, because great employees tend to make you look good as a leader. Thus, if you want to achieve your own exemplary performance in the workplace, place a priority on developing your employees to the exemplary level, and you will enjoy the benefits that result.

Managing Your Time

In addition to maintaining your motivation by focusing on the benefits of using the model, you will need to clear time on your schedule to fit performance development into your day-to-day work. You can free up time by delegating some tasks to others, adding some time to your own workday, or working performance development into your regular meetings with your employees.

Note that performance development is a continual, ongoing process, so it really needs to become a "way of life" for you—or more aptly a "way of work"—rather than just a bunch of singular tasks on your to-do list or calendar. Thus, not only do you need to work regularly scheduled performance development meetings with your direct reports into your workweek, but you will want to develop a sort of performance development mind-set in which continually coaching your employees to excellence seems natural. The coaching will be done not through advice but through supportive questioning that helps your employees self-assess as well as internalize the development process of targeting strengths, identifying relevant performance factors, and creating and following action plans so that they too build a performance development mind-set.

Leveraging Resources

Another key part of self-management involves becoming an effective "resource connector," by becoming proficient at identifying existing resources and securing, as needed, new resources that you in turn are able to offer to your employees as support for their action plans. Sometimes you will need to become a strong advocate for your employees, lobbying for resources on their behalf from your own leaders; at other times you will need to be clever about bending currently available resources to the needs of your employees. The resources you will secure for your employees will run a wide gamut, depending on the given action plan. To be effective at developing employee performance, you will need to become proficient at making use of all of the resources available to you—securing and sharing them.

Interestingly, in many cases, leaders have the very resources they need already available to them; they simply don't make the time or commitment to follow through and leverage those resources. Some common reasons that people don't take advantage of resources that are currently available to them include the following:

- People are hesitant to cut into their budget to fund resources out of fiscal fear or just on principle. They have the unfounded belief that it's not worth spending money on development or that there isn't enough money to spend on development, without any real evidence to back up this belief.

- People create phantom rules that don't really exist, thinking, "I can't ask for this resource" or, "The organization won't support me in obtaining this resource." In these cases, people are operating on the basis of conjecture rather than actually investigating whether they will be able to secure the desired resources.

- People are busy and don't set aside time to obtain resources.

I recommend that you not make resource decisions on the basis of fear or unfounded beliefs. Instead of assuming that your department can't afford certain resources or that your leadership won't authorize the use of certain resources, investigate to see whether that is actually the case. You may be surprised to discover that you *can* obtain the desired resources. If not, you can then turn to plan B, in which you get creative about helping your employees leverage and develop performance.

AVOIDING PITFALLS DURING THE FOUR STEPS OF THE EXEMPLARY PERFORMANCE MODEL

In addition to the more general challenges of working performance development into your leadership role, you will want to look out for a handful of specific challenges when using the Exemplary Performance Model. These are summarized in table 18.

TABLE 18 Challenges and Solutions for Working with the Model

STEP	CHALLENGE	DIAGNOSTIC QUESTION	SOLUTION
0*	Avoid following your gut when assessing performance; instead, rely on a specific job profile and measures of the employee's current performance.	Do I have the employee's written job profile on hand that includes the tasks, knowledge, skills, abilities, behaviors, standards, and metrics required for success in that job? Have I measured current employee performance?	If not, (a) create a job profile that contains the tasks, knowledge, skills, abilities, behaviors, standards, and metrics required for success in that job as well as (b) measures of the employee's current level of performance.
1	Work to identify a strength that is truly expandable.	Is there really room for significant improvement?	If not, search for other expandable strengths.
1	Target strengths that are truly important and impactful.	Is the return on expectations for this task worth the time, effort, and resources?	If not, target a different strength, one that has strong importance to departmental goals and is expected to lead to significant results (impact).
2	Identify the *key* factor responsible for performance.	Does the selected factor play the biggest role in the targeted strength being exemplary or expandable?	If you are unsure, make your best effort (in collaboration with the employee) to determine the factor that will yield the biggest payoffs if leveraged or developed.
3	Design an action plan that is *specific* and *measurable*.	Once this action plan is complete, will I be able to measure the results?	If not, reformulate action items to be more specific and measurable.
4	Follow through on completing the action items assigned to you.	Have I done everything I have promised I'd do to support the employee's action plan?	If not, make a plan for getting your tasks done and set aside time to do so.

* This is a prerequisite to using the model and not a formal step in the process.

ADOPTING THE RIGHT LEADERSHIP STYLE

As mentioned earlier, part of becoming successful at performance development is learning to reenvision your role as a leader as primarily being a developer of people rather than just as an executor of strategy. In other words, you will be developing people (first) in the service of executing strategy (second). Integrating the use of the Exemplary Performance Model into your work life may also involve you making a fundamental shift in your leadership style, not just your leadership role. If you are one of those who tend to lead by exception—that is, intervening with employees only when something goes wrong and trusting the status quo the rest of the time—adopting the present model will involve becoming a leader who proactively and continually engages employees to assess and tweak performance, regardless of how well things are going day-to-day. Instead of being a reactive leader—putting out fires when they come up—you will transform into a proactive leader who regularly supports employees in the development process such that fires are less likely to happen and that the whole team is better equipped to deal with crises when they arise. You will discover that the more you proactively develop people, the less you will have to discipline them, because development is a positive motivator for high performance.

As you can see, at each step of the development process, there are different challenges you will aim to master.

Fortunately, most of these are not make-or-break challenges. Although meeting each challenge successfully will help you get the most out of using the model, being a little off the mark with any given challenge won't render the model useless. For example, if you identify a performance factor to address that is related to the performance problem but not ultimately the factor *most responsible* for performance, you may still see some positive results from your action plan. In addition, once you realize that another performance factor is playing an important role, you can simply adjust the action plan to accommodate that realization. Since the performance development process is ongoing, not finite, you will have plenty of opportunities to make adjustments and engage in fine-tuning along the way.

Using the Model for Organizational Initiatives

The Exemplary Performance Model can also be adapted for use at the organizational level, rather than at the individual level. That is, instead of focusing on developing individual performance to the exemplary level, you can use the model to determine which organizational initiatives to invest in and how each initiative should be structured. To do so, you would adapt the model in the following way:

1. **Assess and target performance**—Develop a list of the organization's key performance metrics (e.g., turnover) and measure the current performance on each. Compare current performance (e.g., 15 percent turnover) to desired performance (e.g., 12 percent turnover) to determine whether each of the key outcomes is exemplary (best-in-class) or expandable (below best-in-class).

2. **Diagnose cause(s) of performance**—Determine the cause (key performance factor most responsible) for each current key outcome.

3. **Develop and implement a plan**—Develop an action plan (initiative) for each current key outcome that applies the right tool(s) to leverage the exemplary outcome (possibly take advantage of it in a different way) and the right tool(s) to develop the expandable outcome.

4. **Follow up**—Follow up to see how the process is working to leverage and develop the targeted areas and adjust the action plan as needed.

Next Steps

I will leave you with a few tips for moving the Exemplary Performance Model from theory to practice. Once you are ready to engage in the

WHEN THE LEADER IS THE ROADBLOCK

Sometimes the biggest challenge of all may involve recognizing when you as a leader may be an obstacle to an employee's development. Most of us want to empower our employees to be successful, yet we may not be able—whether owing to our blind spots or an unwillingness to accept responsibility—to recognize or acknowledge areas where we are holding up development. Truth be told, leaders can play a role in holding back performance in a way that touches on any one of the possible performance factors, whether because of not communicating clear expectations, not being willing to provide needed equipment, not supporting the employee to take time for training, and so forth. If you and the employee get stuck at any step of the development process, take some time to look inward and reflect on the role you might be playing in the employee's performance. The issue here isn't one of guilt or blame; the goal is to simply unblock the process and keep moving forward. The good news is that once you identify roadblocks to performance that may be connected to your leadership, you will have the knowledge and power to *make changes*—to empower your employee to become exemplary and, in turn, to empower your organization to do the same.

process of developing performance—to take what you've learned in these pages and apply that learning to the real world—here are the first steps you can follow to get the process moving:

- Solicit buy-in for the model from top leadership (always important).

- Create or revise job profiles, if needed, to include the level of depth required to serve as the foundation for using the model (see chapter 2 for more information).

- Determine how you will train people in your organization to use the model (When? Where? How? By whom?).

- Rework your schedule to provide the time needed to begin using the model.

- Continually work to create a trusting environment at work.

All of these tasks will help you get the performance development process moving and can go a long way toward helping make the process successful. In particular, as noted earlier in this chapter as well as earlier in the book, buy-in from your top leadership—while not a deal breaker for using this model—will go a long way toward helping you successfully integrate this model into your organization. When use of the model is sanctioned, it is easier to designate time for performance development as well as to obtain the resources needed to support the process. As has been highlighted throughout the book, the job profile is a major prerequisite for using the model, because it provides the tasks and performance standards that will be used to assess performance (step 1). In addition, before using the model, people—leaders and employees alike—will need some training on how to use the model. Since you and others in your organization may never have used the model before, training will help improve everyone's knowledge and skill on how to implement the model. Exemplary performance development can happen only if you set aside the time to use the model and follow through on the action plans generated by it. Finally, people will self-assess and actively participate only if they trust that the model is truly about development and not about catching them doing something wrong. As a result, you will want to work continuously to build trust with your employees.

Conclusion: The Rewards of Using the Model

In the short term, by using the Exemplary Performance Model, you will foster high morale and motivation in your employees. The power of giving your employees the kind of attention endorsed by this model is substantial for keeping employees engaged in their work. In the long-term, by using the Exemplary Performance Model, you will foster exemplary performance across your team. As your employees become better and better at achieving their goals, the organization too will become better at achieving its stated strategy (assuming performance goals are aligned with larger strategic initiatives). In short, exemplary employees make for exemplary organizations.

Successful use of the Exemplary Performance Model tends to build employees' sense of confidence and self-efficacy. As employees internalize the model and discover that they are in fact capable of exemplary performance, the benefits of the model tend to expand. Employees often start using the model on their own, continually self-assessing to fine-tune their own performance, becoming better and better at what they do. And, interestingly, when employees demonstrate excellence, they typically don't resort to resting on their laurels afterward; instead, they typically work hard to maintain their position of excellence. Most people simply don't want to be knocked off the top of the totem pole. So the Exemplary Performance Model is a powerful tool for yielding high performance, and once high performance is achieved, it tends to beget more high performance.

You can witness the power of this model yourself. No matter what kind of organization you work in—small or large, entrepreneurial or traditional, technical or nontechnical—the Exemplary Performance Model has the potential to serve as a powerful tool for achieving excellence, one person at a time. You too, as someone who now knows how to help employees reach the exemplary level, will reach exemplary performance yourself, in one of your key roles: developing people. In the end, using the Exemplary Performance Model with your employees will help you create an engaged team of effective strategy executors, ultimately distinguishing your organization from the competition. With the Exemplary Performance Model as a resource, excellence is completely attainable!

Exemplary Performance Model Increases Sales at City Furniture

Although I have implemented the Exemplary Performance Model many times over the years, until now it has not been possible to examine its effectiveness in a study where I could control many of the variables that affect performance. For example, one organization rolled out the model to an entire department, but we could not compare the results in that department with a similar department that did not implement the model.

However, in a case study specifically conducted for this book, at City Furniture in Florida we were able to do a more controlled examination of whether or not the model is effective. We were able to roll out the model in a way that controlled for other variables by having a continuous control group: a showroom that did not have the model rolled out but was very similar to the showroom that did.

The study showroom's average monthly sales per employee increased 27.11 percent more than those of the control showroom.

Through this study, we will begin to see how quickly an organization can achieve meaningful results through using the model to leverage and develop people's strengths. As you will see, in comparing the sales increases in each showroom during the two months after training, the study showroom's average monthly sales per employee increased 27.11 percent more than those of the control showroom.

Background

City Furniture is a midsize furniture retailer operating fifteen showrooms throughout South Florida. Established in 1971, the organization was originally named Waterbed City. In 1990 the company expanded its product line to include innerspring mattresses and home furnishings. It changed its name to City Furniture in 1994, reflecting the expanded focus into mid- to upper-market furniture. Today, as in the past, the company provides quality home furnishings at excellent values and focuses on customer service, efficiency, and a fun and friendly culture. Additionally, City Furniture is the only South Florida furniture store that provides same-day delivery. This service provides a major competitive advantage.

In 2004, City Furniture decided to compete in the low-cost furniture market and licensed six Ashley Furniture stores. In doing so, City Furniture was able to leverage its infrastructure to provide Ashley Furniture's customers with same-day delivery of furniture purchased by 3:00 p.m. By the end of 2008, City Furniture will have three additional licenses for Ashley Furniture stores.

I originally worked with City Furniture in 2007 to develop a strategic talent management road map, working with Curt Nichols, vice president of Human Resources, and Janet Wincko, director of training. Curt has been with City Furniture for sixteen years, starting as a sales associate and moving through the organization into his current role. Janet has been with City Furniture for eighteen years, starting as an HR generalist.

As I began assessing talent management practices, it became clear that performance management would be a major area of focus. After seeing a presentation on the Exemplary Performance Model, Curt and Janet started discussions about implementing the model at City Furniture.

Rolling Out the Model

To implement the model, I partnered with Curt and Janet to develop a rollout plan. We decided to start with a pilot study, applying the model with the employees at one showroom. Starting the rollout at one location would help us determine whether the model was effective at improving the performance of sales associates, before introducing it throughout the entire company. We planned to measure sales on a weekly basis for two months before the training and implementation and for two months after it.

It was also determined that we would measure sales at another showroom during those same weeks, creating a control group. This second showroom was to be of a similar geographic location, size, and sales volume as the showroom where we were rolling out the model. However, the model would not be implemented at the second showroom.

We chose the Pompano Beach showroom as the location where we would pilot the model—the study location. This showroom was chosen on the basis of proximity to the corporate headquarters and because of the availability of another showroom of similar size and volume in the same geographic area. We chose the Fort Lauderdale showroom to serve as our continuous control group. Although the Fort Lauderdale location is only 4.7 miles from Pompano Beach, the leaders in the two showrooms do not interact, so the control showroom's leaders would not become aware of the model.

One difference between the showrooms was the number of sales associates at each facility. The Pompano Beach showroom had seven sales associates and two managers who were also responsible for selling as a major part of their job profile. The Fort Lauderdale showroom had thirteen sales associates and two managers. This difference was accounted for by tracking average sales per sales associate per month for the project.

After these decisions were made, Janet and I had a phone conversation with Jamie Bowen, general manager of the Pompano Beach showroom. During this conversation, we communicated our plans to conduct the training at his location, provided an overview of the model and how it worked, and asked if he and his staff of two sales supervisors would be willing to participate. He was very willing and seemed excited to be chosen.

Janet and I trained Jamie and his two showroom managers on how to use the model. The training was conducted over the course of four hours and included a detailed review of the model, a demonstration of the model, and role-plays by the participants. During the final role-play, each participant demonstrated the use of the model, where I acted as the employee. Participants were given feedback throughout the process to let them know what they did well and what they could do differently to be more effective. Janet and I then discussed our perceptions of the readiness of each person to use the model and determined that each person could successfully use the model with their associates.

On a monthly basis, Janet and I checked in with Jamie to get his feedback and provide support. This proved to be a valuable tool in ensuring that the project was moving forward and did not lose momentum. For example, in the first check-in, we learned that the sales supervisors were not applying the model themselves. They were focused on selling and meeting quota, and Jamie was using the model with each individual salesperson. Jamie felt that this was important for two reasons. First, he felt it would show his support and get the attention of each salesperson by implementing the model himself. And, second, this allowed the showroom managers to focus on meeting their sales quotas, which were part of their compensation plans.

Outcomes

Sales were tracked for each location during the two months prior to training and the two months after training. The data were gathered from January 12 through April 30, 2008.

QUANTITATIVE FINDINGS

The first metric we examined was average monthly sales difference per employee for each month (see table 1). The "difference" denotes a comparison between the Pompano Beach (study) and Fort Lauderdale (control) showrooms. We chose to examine monthly data due to great variability in daily and weekly sales for both showrooms. We then compared the average monthly difference between showrooms for the two months before the model was implemented to the two months after.

As can be seen in table 1, sales associates in the Pompano Beach showroom sold a greater dollar amount of products on average than sales associates in the Fort Lauderdale showroom, regardless of the month we examined. Table 1 also shows the average difference between showrooms before and after the model was implemented. In the two months before the model was implemented, the Pompano Beach showroom sold an average of $12,042.27 per sales associate per month more than the Fort Lauderdale showroom. In the month the model was rolled out and the month after, the difference jumped by 27.11 per-

TABLE 1 **Difference Between Study and Control Locations in Average Sales per Employee per Month**

MONTH	DIFFERENCE IN SALES PER EMPLOYEE: STUDY OVER CONTROL LOCATION	TWO-MONTH AVERAGE DIFFERENCE: STUDY OVER CONTROL LOCATION	PERIOD OF THE STUDY
January	+$17,982.96	+$12,042.27	Before Training
February	+$6,101.58		
March	+$25,340.13	+$15,307.50	After Training
April	+$5,274.87		
		+$3,265.23	Difference between two months before and two months after
		+27.11%	Percentage difference

cent to $15,307.50 per sales associate. This accounts for an increase of $3,265.23 per sales associate per month.

QUALITATIVE FINDINGS

In our initial check-in, Jamie reported success as soon as he began using the model. He felt that the model was easy to use, flowed well, and was well received by each salesperson. He stated that people liked it because they wanted to improve their performance, and the model gave them the opportunity to do so in a focused way. He was excited at being able to have one particular employee share his exemplary strength with the team. This exemplary strength, communicating orders back to customers, was an expandable strength for some of the other associates and a weakness for a few people. And one person in particular focused on an expandable strength of selling in-home service agreements and made his sales quota by the second week. In the previous two months, he had fallen short of quota in that area.

In our check-in at the end of the second month after implementing the model, Jamie stated that the model had proved to be simple to use and effective and that the simplicity did not reduce the model's impact. The main benefits were that it focused on strengths that proved to be motivational, that it allowed him to help his salespeople leverage exemplary strengths and develop expandable strengths, and that once they learned the model, the conversations didn't take long. After the training, he understood how to use the model well and felt confident using it. He felt that he wasn't struggling with the process, and his salespeople enjoyed the process and were more engaged than before.

Analysis and Discussion

The data make clear that the model was effective in improving sales performance. The two showrooms that were compared were in close proximity and had the same customer base. Marketing was done on a regional scale and was not specific to any showroom. Any sales incentives and additional sales training was available equally to both showrooms. The showrooms did not talk with each other, so there was no carryover of the training between showrooms. It is reasonable to conclude that the results were a function of the implementation and use of the model. It was the only significant variable that was different between showrooms.

Given the similarities between locations, Pompano Beach's increase in average monthly sales per employee of 27.11 percent over the Fort Lauderdale showroom is impressive. Since all other conditions were relatively equal, this increase is most likely due to the implementation and continued use of the model.

Additionally, an average increase of $3,265.23 per person per month is meaningful to the bottom line of the organization. This equates to $176,592.96 in additional revenue per year for the Pompano Beach showroom. Considering the minimal costs of training and time involved, the return on investment is high.

There were also lessons learned in rolling out the model at City Furniture. First and foremost, Jamie said that if he had it to do over again, he would announce the rollout in a group meeting to help his salespeople understand what he was doing and set expectations, and to allay the fear people felt in meeting with Jamie in his office in the middle of the month. He also feels that the model will have an even greater impact with new salespeople, who will learn quickly that he is there to help develop their sales skills so that they can be successful. Jamie feels that it is important for leaders to take the time to use the Exemplary Performance Model with their employees. Doing so sends a message that the employees' performance is important and that you have an interest in their success.

We should note that the time period examined after the rollout of the model was short (two months). You would expect to see results over time and not such marked results out of the gate because development does not happen overnight. Judging from Jamie's feedback, we can see that a level of excitement was created by using the model. This excitement may have increased people's motivation and caused them to perform at higher levels. However, the specific cause of the immediate improvement was not determined.

After examining all the results (quantitative and qualitative), we can see that the model was clearly effective at the Pompano Beach showroom of City Furniture. This result aligns with my previous experience in using the model at other organizations. Through leveraging and developing strengths, employees become more engaged in the development, leaders gain better-performing employees, and the organization is more likely to achieve its goals. To quote Jamie, "If you're there for them, they'll be there for you."

Questions for Use in Diagnosing Performance Factors

FACTOR	DIAGNOSTIC QUESTIONS EXEMPLARY STRENGTH	DIAGNOSTIC QUESTIONS EXPANDABLE STRENGTH
Talent and Fit	1. Does the employee exhibit *superior* physical traits, intellectual ability, and personality characteristics for success at this task? 2. Does the employee display *exceptional* passion and preference for working on this task? 3. Does the employee display *exceptional* passion and preference for the organizational culture and values?	1. Does the employee exhibit the physical traits, intellectual ability, and personality characteristics needed to be successful at this task? 2. Does the employee display passion and preference for working on this type of task? 3. Does the employee display passion and preference for the organizational culture and values?
Environment	1. Are there internal or external events occuring that have a *positive* impact on the employee's performance? 2. Does the employee's physical work setting have a positive impact on performance? 3. Could something happening in the employee's personal life be having a positive impact on the employee's performance?	1. Are there internal or external events occuring that are having a *negative* impact on the employee's ability to perform at the exemplary level? 2. Does the employee's physical *work setting* negatively affect performance? 3. Could something happening outside of work be affecting the employee's ability to perform at the exemplary level?

FACTOR	DIAGNOSTIC QUESTIONS EXEMPLARY STRENGTH	DIAGNOSTIC QUESTIONS EXPANDABLE STRENGTH
Tools and Resources	1. Does the employee have tools that are *superior* to those used by other performers for the given task? 2. Does the employee have resources that are *superior* to those used by other performers for the given task?	1. Does the employee have the tools needed to execute the task at the exemplary level? 2. Does the employee have the resources needed to execute the task at the exemplary level? 3. If the employee were given additional tools or resources, would exemplary performance be more likely?
Systems and Processes	1. Does the employee consistently follow a process when completing the targeted task? 2. Is the process used by the exemplary employee *superior* to the process used by others?	1. Does the employee consistently follow a process when completing the targeted task? 2. Does the employee use a process that is *different* from the process used by an exemplar? 3. Does the *recommended* process appear to be broken or faulty?
Clear Expectations and Accountability	NA (This factor will not be the reason for the exemplary strength.)	1. Have clear expectations been described for the employee? 2. Are the expectations for the employee and leader the same? 3. Is the employee consistently held accountable for performance?

FACTOR	DIAGNOSTIC QUESTIONS EXEMPLARY STRENGTH	DIAGNOSTIC QUESTIONS EXPANDABLE STRENGTH
Knowledge and Skills	1. Does the employee demonstrate significantly *greater knowledge* regarding the given task? 2. Does the employee demonstrate significantly *greater skill* in the given task?	1. If the employee had to, could he or she perform the task at a higher level than is currently the case? 2. Has the employee performed this task at the exemplary level at any time in the past? 3. Will further improvement of knowledge or skills be likely to improve the employee's performance?
Motivation	1. Are the rewards for a given task *valued more* by the employee or considered to be *more sufficient* by the employee? 2. Does the employee feel that there is a higher probability of receiving the rewards for completing a given task than do other employees? 3. Does the employee feel that there is a higher probability of achieving the level of performance necessary to receive the rewards than do other employees?	1. Are the rewards for doing a given task valued by the employee and considered to be sufficient? 2. Does the employee feel that there is a high probability of receiving the rewards for a given task? 3. Does the employee feel that there is a high probability of achieving the level of performance necessary to receive the rewards?

Notes

Introduction

1. Harold Stolovitch and Erica Keeps, *Handbook of Human Performance Technology* (San Francisco: Jossey-Bass, 1992).

2. Robert F. Manger and Peter Pipe, *Analyzing Performance Problems,* 3d ed. (Atlanta: Center for Effective Performance, 1997).

3. Thomas F. Gilbert, *Human Competence: Engineering Worthy Performance* (New York: McGraw-Hill, 1978).

4. Marcus Buckingham, *Go Put Your Strengths to Work: 6 Powerful Steps to Achieve Outstanding Performance* (New York: The Free Press, 2007).

5. Stolovich and Keeps, *Handbook of Human Performance Technology.*

6. Buckingham, *Go Put Your Strengths to Work.*

7. Ibid.

8. Larry Bossidy and Ram Charan, *Execution: The Discipline of Getting Things Done* (New York: Crown Business, 2002), 5.

9. Robert S. Kaplan and David P. Norton, *The Strategy-Focused Organization: How Balanced Scorecard Companies Thrive in the New Business Environment* (Cambridge, MA: Harvard Business School Publishing, 2001), 1.

Chapter 1

1. I am not referring to "significance" in the statistical sense but rather as a way of denoting a noticeably large performance differential.

2. Stanley Eitzen, "Upward Mobility Through Sport? The Myths and Realities," http://www.zmag.org/zmag/articles/mar99eitzen.htm, from *Fair and Foul: Beyond the Myths and Paradoxes of Sport,* 2d ed. (Lanham, MD: Rowman & Littlefield, 2003).

3. "The Best Places to Launch a Career: The Top 50 Employers for New College Grads," *BusinessWeek* (September 18, 2006).

4. According to Morningstar.com, Disney stock went from $16.85 a share on February 1, 2003, to $32.19 a share on February 1, 2008.

5. Edwin A. Locke and Gary P. Latham, "Building a Practically Useful Theory of Goal Setting and Task Motivation: A 35 Year Odyssey," *American Psychologist* (September 2002), 705–17.

6. "World Record Progression for the Mile Run," http://en.wikipedia.org /wiki/World_record_progression_for_the_mile_run.

7. See Stephen Covey's *Seven Habits of Highly Effective People* (New York: The Free Press, 2004) for more information on the value of understanding one's locus of control.

8. Marcus Buckingham, *Go Put Your Strengths to Work: 6 Powerful Steps to Achieve Outstanding Performance* (New York: The Free Press, 2007).

Chapter 2

1. Marcus Buckingham and Donald Clifton, *Now, Discover Your Strengths* (New York: Simon & Schuster Trade, 2001).

2. Tom Rath, Strengths Finder 2.0: *A New and Updated Edition of the Online Test from Gallup's Now, Discover Your Strengths* (New York: Gallup Press, 2007).

3. John C. Maxwell, *Failing Forward: How to Make the Most of Your Mistakes* (Nashville, TN: Thomas Nelson, 2000).

Chapter 3

1. For a review of the literature on the link between talent and performance, see James W. Westerman and Bret L. Simmons, "The Effects of Work Environment on the Personality–Performance Relationship: An Exploratory Study," *Journal of Managerial Issues* (summer 2007). http://www.entrepreneur.com/tradejournals/article/166092745.html.

2. Chad Zimmerman, "How Michael Became His Airness: How Michael Jordan's 'Breakfast Club' Helped the Chicago Bulls Win 6 Titles," *Stack* (summer 2006). This article can also be found online. See http://www .maxpreps.com/FanPages/Content/Article.mxp/ArticleID-21539c5a-c29c-4572-a4a6-d15e01cb83af.

3. For a more complete description of selection testing, see Robert L. Mathis and John H. Jackson, *Human Resource Management,* 12th ed. (Mason, OH: Thomson South-Western, 2008), 237–40.

4. Thomas Rollins and Darryl Roberts, *Work Culture, Organizational Performance, and Business Success: Measurement and Management* (Westport, CT: Quorum Books, 1998); Douglas N. Ross, "Does Corporate Culture Contribute to Performance?" *American International College Journal of Business* (2000).

Chapter 4

1. Jacqueline C. Vishcer, "The Effects of the Physical Environment on Job Performance: Towards a Theoretical Model of Workspace Stress," *Stress and Health* 23, no. 3, 175–84.

2. Gareth Morgan, *Images of Organization* (Thousand Oaks, CA: Sage Publications, 1997), 116–17.

3. See, for example, Human Synergistics International, "Impact of Organisational Culture on Sales Performance" (Sydney, Australia: Human Synergistics International). www.human-synergistics.com.au/content/apps/get-kms-document.asp?ID=5240&ContentType=pdf.

4. Rodd Wagner and James K. Harter, *12: The Elements of Great Managing* (New York: Gallup Press, 2006).

5. Peter A. Hancock, "Human Performance and Ergonomics," in *Handbook of Perception and Cognition,* 2d ed., ed. Peter A. Hancock (San Diego, CA: Academic Press, 1999).

6. MIT Sloan Management, "Bridging the Work-Family Divide," http://mitsloan.mit.edu/newsroom/2006-bailyn.php.

7. Rabi S. Bhagat, "Effects of Stressful Life Events on Individual Performance Effectiveness and Work Adjustment Processes Within Organizational Settings: A Research Model," *Academy of Management Review* 8, no. 4 (October 1983), 660–71.

8. Charles A. Czeisler and Bronwyn Fryer, "Sleep Deficit: The Performance Killer," *Harvard Business Review* 84, no. 10 (October 2006), 53–59.

9. Corporate Leadership Council, "Driving Performance and Retention Through Employee Engagement" (Corporate Leadership Council, 2004). http://www.mckpeople.com.au/SiteMedia/w3svc161/Uploads/Documents/760af459-93b3-43c7-b52a-2a74e984c1a0.pdf.

Chapter 6

1. Thomas Pyzdek, *The Six Sigma Handbook: A Complete Guide for Green Belts, Black Belts, and Managers at All Levels* (New York: McGraw-Hill Professional, 2003).

2. Ibid.

Chapter 7

1. Oscar G. Mink, Keith Q. Owen, and Barbara P. Mink, *Developing High-Performance People: The Art of Coaching* (Reading, MA: Addison-Wesley, 1993), 57.

2. The Gallup Organization, "Q12 Element: Q01," MSQ12Brf_01.SND.Ws. ENUS04.04.07 (Princeton, NJ, 2007). www.gallupuniversity.com.

3. Lee Roy Beach, *The Human Element: Understanding and Managing Employee Behavior* (Armonk, NY: M. E. Sharpe, Inc, 2007).

4. Harry E. Chambers and Robert Craft, *No Fear Management: Rebuilding Trust, Performance, and Commitment in the New American Workplace* (Boca Raton: CRC Press, 1998), 130.

5. John S. Adams, "Inequity in Social Exchange," *Advances in Experimental Social Psychology* 62 (1965), 335–43.

6. Jo Manion, "Nurture a Culture of Retention," *Nursing Management* 35, no. 4 (2004), 29–39.

7. J. M. Harackiewicz, C. Sansone, and G. Manderlink, "Competence, Achievement Orientation, and Intrinsic Motivation: A Process Analysis," *Journal of Personality and Social Psychology* 48, no. 2 (1985), 493–508; R. M. Steers and L. W. Porter, "The Role of Task-Goal Attributes in Employee Performance," *Psychological Bulletin* 81 (1974), 434–52.

8. Aubrey C. Daniels, *Performance Management: Improving Quality Productivity Through Positive Reinforcement*, 3d ed. (Atlanta: Performance Management Publications, 1989), 190.

9. The Gallup Organization, "Q12 Element."

Chapter 8

1. International Coach Federation, "Frequently Asked Questions About Coaching" (2008). http://www.coachfederation.org/ICF/For+Coaching+Client

s/What+is+a+Coach/FAQs.

Chapter 9

1. Kenneth W. Thomas, *Intrinsic Motivation at Work: Building Energy and Commitment* (San Francisco: Berrett-Koehler Publishing, 2002), 6–9.

2. V. H. Vroom, *Work and Motivation* (New York: Wiley, 1964).

3. Bill W. George and Peter E. Sims, *True North: Discover Your Authentic Leadership* (San Francisco: Jossey-Bass, 2007), 106.

4. Edward L. Deci and Richard M. Ryan, *Intrinsic Motivation and Self-Determination in Human Behavior* (New York: Plenum Press, 1985), 35.

5. For example, D. J. Campbell and D. R. Ilgen, "Additive Effects of Task Difficulty and Goal Setting on Subsequent Performance," *Journal of Applied Psychology* 61 (1976), 319–24.

Chapter 11

1. If your employer explicitly requests that you do not spend time on performance development, I am not recommending you go against your employer's wishes.

Index

A

ability, 146
accountability: consistent administration of, 129; definition of, 33; description of, 17; of employee, 132; examples of, 128; goal of, 130; lack of, 129; performance affected by, 139; positive performance promotion through, 128–129; punishment vs., 130. *See also* clear expectations and accountability
achievement, 169
action plan: creation of, 34–36; description of, 13; development of, 187–189, 207; elements of, 34; follow-up, 191; goal of, 187; implementation of, 187–189, 207; review of, 190
appreciation, 167
aptitude assessments, 51
assessment: performance, 30–31; talent and fit, 51–54, 63
at-standards performance, 7–8, 58

B

behavior modeling, 150
"below-exemplary" performance, 15–16
benchmarking, 176–177
benefits, 78

best practices, 135–136
brain function, 52–53

C

check-in meetings, 36
clear expectations and accountability: best-practices list, 135–136; case study of, 137–138; clear expectations, 123–127; coaching for addressing of, 135; communication of, 137; competency models, 135–136; consequences, 125; definition of, 33, 122–130; delivery of, to employee, 131–132; description of, 121–122; exemplary strengths and, 133; expandable strength and, 130–136; feedback for addressing of, 134–135; goal setting, 136; job profile, 136; leader's expectations correlated with employee's expectations, 132; leveraging of exemplary strength, 136–137; motivation factor and, 129; performance affected by, 138–139; productivity affected by, 139; questions for diagnosing, 220; responsibility for addressing, 137; setting of, 131; summary of, 138–139. *See also* accountability

client meeting space, 98
climate in workplace, 70–71
coaching, 36, 135, 150–151, 153, 203
communication: of clear
    expectations, 133–134;
    description of, 79; of
    expectations, 137; importance of,
    38; with people, 92
competency models, 135–136
consequences, 125
creative workarounds, 96–98
culture. *See* organizational culture
current performance, 30–31
cutting-edge performance, 10

D
development: of performance. *See*
    performance development;
    training and, 13–14
documentation, 195–196

E
Eitzen, Stanley, 9
employee(s): accountability of, 132;
    blaming of, 5, 14; capability to
    perform at a higher level,
    146–147; clear expectations
    discussed with, 131–132;
    feedback from, 116; financial
    assistance and planning, 79; lack
    of motivation, 20; morale of, 209;
    negative conduct by, 18;
    performance development of,
    13–15; performing of tasks at
    high levels, 147; processes
    followed by, 108–109; refusal to
    participate in development
    process, 20; self-assessment by,
    99; self-confidence of, 209;
    strategic execution affected by,
    4–5; tools and resources access,
    93–94; training of, 16
employee assistance programs,
    76–77, 79
employee benefits, 78

empowerment, 167
environment: case study of, 84–85;
    definition of, 33, 65–66; employee
    assistance programs, 76–77, 79;
    exemplary strength and, 74–75,
    80–81; expandable strength and,
    73–74; job reassignment or
    transfer, 77–78; leader's role in
    promoting, 82–83; leveraging of
    performance related to, 76–81;
    personal, 71–73; plan to work
    around in challenges in, 83–84;
    questions for diagnosing, 219;
    responsibility for addressing,
    81–84; summary of, 85; tools for
    addressing, 76–78, 80–81; work.
    See work environment;
    workplace assessment and
    redesign, 77
exemplary performance: description
    of, 8–10; as development goal,
    15–16; follow-up, 16–17, 36–37;
    reinforcement, 16–17; strengths-
    based focus and, 16
Exemplary Performance Model:
    applications of, 20–21; areas not
    helped by, 18–20; case study of,
    211–217; challenges for, 197–207;
    development discussions,
    195–196; foundational principles
    of, 11–17; leadership buy-in,
    198–200; levels of performance,
    7–10; metrics, 5–6; organizational
    buy-in, 38; organizational
    initiatives addressed with, 207;
    pitfalls in, 204–207; prerequisites
    for using, 38–39; real-world uses
    of, 61–62, 84–85, 100–101,
    118–119, 137–138, 154, 170–171;
    returns on investment, 11; review
    of, 175–176; rewards of using,
    209–210; standards, 6–7; steps in,
    24–25, 30–37, 175–176, 191–196;
    target employees for, 19; targeted-
    areas focus of, 20, 25; tools of, 35
exemplary performers, 108

exemplary strengths: clear
expectations and accountability
factor as key to, 133; definition of,
27; diagnosing causes of, 183–186;
environment factor as key to,
74–75; expandable strengths and,
194–195; knowledge and skills
factor as key to, 148–149;
leveraging of, 30, 60; motivation
and, 163–164; performance
factors, 31, 56, 185; strengths
classified into, 178–180; systems
and processes factor as key to,
110; talent and fit factor as key to,
56–57; targeting of, 180–183; tools
and resources factor as key to,
94–95
expandable strengths, 16; clear
expectations and accountability
factor as key to, 130–136;
communication of information
for development of, 133–134;
description of, 27–28;
development of, 96, 119;
diagnosing causes of, 184,
186–187; environment as key to,
73–74, 80–81; exemplary
strengths and, 194–195;
knowledge and skills factor as
key to, 145–152; leveraging of. *See*
leveraging of strengths;
motivation as key to, 158;
performance factors associated
with, 31, 186–187; strengths
classified into, 178–180; systems
and processes as key to, 107–109;
talent and fit as key to, 50–56;
targeting of, 180–183; tools and
resources as key to, 92–94, 96
extremely poor performance, 18–19
extrinsic motivation, 156

F
faulty processes, 109
feedback, 116, 122, 134–135
financial assistance and planning, 79

financial resources, 90, 93, 98
fit. *See* talent and fit
follow-up, 16–17, 36–37, 189–191,
207
formal processes, 105–107
fulfillment, 167

G
General Aptitude Test Battery, 52
goals: creating of, 188–189; setting
of, 136, 169

H
hard skills, 144
hiring of employees, 51

I
informal processes, 105–107
information resource, 92, 93
intangible rewards, 156, 159–160,
165–167
interpersonal relationships, 68–69
intrinsic motivation, 156

J
job description, 37
job profile: creation of, 192;
definition of, 37–38; expectations
for employee conveyed in, 136;
organizational strategy and, 200;
restructuring of, 58, 62; reviewing
with employee, 131
job reassignment, 77–78
job transfer or termination, 59, 77–78

K
knowledge and skills: case study of,
154; citing of, 145; coaching,
150–151, 153; definition of, 33,
142–145; description of, 141;
exemplary strength and, 148–149;
expandable strength and,
145–152; hard skills, 144;
improvement of, 147–148;
leader's role in addressing, 152;
leveraging of exemplary

knowledge and skills *(cont.)*
strengths, 152; performance
affected by, 143; questions for
assessing and diagnosing,
145–146, 221; researching, 150,
153; responsibility for addressing,
152; role modeling, 150, 153; soft
skills, 144; stretch assignments,
151–153; summary of, 154; talent
and, 142–143; tools, 149–152, 153;
training effects, 149–150, 153

L
lagging performance, 7, 14
leader: clear expectations provided
by, 127, 137; expectations of, 132;
as obstacle to employee
development, 208; positive
environment fostered by, 82–83;
strategic execution by, 3
leadership: buy-in by, 198–200, 209;
style of, 206
Lean, 115, 117
less-than-exemplary performance,
58
leveraging of resources, 203–204
leveraging of strengths: clear
expectations and accountability,
136–137; description of, 29–30, 60;
environment, 76–81; knowledge
and skills factor, 152; motivation,
169; systems and processes, 116;
tools and resources, 97

M
measurement, 188–189
metrics, performance, 5–6
Minnesota Multiphasic Personality
Inventory, 53
motivation: case study of, 170–171;
clear expectations and
accountability factor, 129;
definition of, 33, 155–157,
171–172; exemplary strength and,
163–164; expandable strength
and, 158; extrinsic, 156; goal

setting, 168; intrinsic, 156;
leveraging of exemplary
strengths, 169; for performance
development, 202–203; as
performance factor, 157–158, 171;
as psychological concept, 171;
questions for diagnosing, 221;
reinforcement survey, 168;
responsible for addressing
strengths related to, 170; rewards
as. *See* rewards; strengths related
to, 158, 163–164, 170; as symptom
vs. cause, 157–158; tools for
developing expandable strength,
164–169; tools to leverage,
169–170

N
negative conduct, 18

O
organization: accountability in, 17;
"bubbling up," 83; changes in, 83;
exemplary performance in, 9;
performance standards in, 15;
reinforcement in, 17; rules of, 107;
talent and fit assessments for
potential employee, 55–56; tasks
aligned with goals of, 201
organizational culture: components
of, 66, 68; definition of, 66;
examples of, 67; performance
affected by, 68; survey of, 76;
talent and fit, 55–56

P
passion, 48, 54–55
performance: accountability effects
on, 128–129, 139; assessment of,
30–31, 177–183, 207; at-standards,
7–8, 58; "below-exemplary,"
15–16; clear expectations and
accountability effects on, 138–139;
collaborative approach to, 194;
constraints on, 73; current, 30–31;
cutting-edge, 10; definition of, 5;

performance *(cont.)*
diagnosing causes of, 183–187, 207; exemplary, 8–10; extremely poor, 18–19; lack of clear expectations effect on, 125; lagging, 7, 14; less-than-exemplary, 58; levels of, 7–10; metrics for assessing, 5–6; organizational culture effects on, 68; physical work setting effects on, 74; returns on investment in, 11; root causes for, 11–13; skills' effect on, 143; standards for assessing, 6–7; strategic execution aligned with, 200–201; targeted areas for improving, 20; targeting of, 30–31
performance development: commitment to, 202–204; goal for, 15–16; importance of, 202–203; individualized approach to, 14–15; as cycle, 25–26; as iterative and parallel process, 25–26; as joint process, 14; ongoing nature of, 206–207; refusal of employee to participate in, 20; resources for, 199–200; time allocation for, 199; time management and, 23–24, 203
performance factors: description of, 31–33; exemplary strengths, 31, 56, 185; expandable strengths, 31; motivation, 157–158, 171; questions for diagnosing, 219–221. *See also specific factor*
personal environment, 71–73
personal style preferences surveys, 51
personality tests, 53
physical work setting, 74
policy manual, 78
praise, 167
preferences, 48–49, 55
process improvement, 111–114, 117
professional network, 79
punishment, 130

R
recognition, 167
reinforcement, 16–17
reinforcement survey, 168
researching, 150, 153
restructuring of job, 58
return on expectations, 181
returns on investment, 11
rewards: determining of, 164–165; intangible, 156, 159–160, 165–167; perceived probability of receiving, 160–162; performance level necessary for receiving, 162–163; standard of performance for, 162; sufficiency of, 158–160; tangible, 156, 159–160, 165–166; valuing of, 158–160
role modeling, 150, 153
rules, 107

S
self-assessments, 38, 99, 192–194
self-management, 203
Six Sigma, 114–115, 117
16 Personality Factors, 53
skills. *See* knowledge and skills
social network, 79
soft skills, 144
standards: exemplary performance and, 8; of performance, 6–7; rewards and, 162; setting of, 15
stimulation, 167
strategic execution: description of, 3; employees and, 4–5; performance alignment with, 200–201
strengths: classification of, 178–180; defining of, 26–27; exemplary. *See* exemplary strengths; exemplary performance reached by focusing on, 16; expandable. *See* expandable strengths; identification of, 178; impact of, 181–183; importance of, 180–183; leveraging of, 29–30; transfer of, 29; value of focusing on, 28
stressful life events, 72

stretch assignments, 151–153
systems and processes: case study of, 118–119; company rules and, 107; definition of, 33, 104–107; description of, 103; exemplary strength and, 110; expandable strength and, 107–109; faulty processes, 109; following of, by employees, 108–109; formal processes, 105–107; informal processes, 105–107; Lean, 115, 117; leveraging the exemplary strength, 116, 119; process improvement, 111–114, 117; processes, 104–107; quality awards, 115; questions for diagnosing, 220; responsibility for addressing, 116–118; Six Sigma, 114–115, 117; summary of, 119; systems, 104; tools to target performance related to, 111–117

T
talent and fit: amount of, 49–50; assessment of, 51–54, 63; brain function, 52–53; components of, 45–47; definition of, 33, 43–45; exemplary strength, 56–57, 60; expandable strength, 50–56; faking of, 47; hiding of, 62; increasing of, 45–46; job transfer or termination because of lack of, 59; lack of, 49, 57–59; motivation vs., 161; organizational culture and values, 55–56; passion, 48, 54–55; personality characteristics, 53; physical traits, 45–46, 52; preferences, 48–49, 55; questions for diagnosing, 219; responsibility for addressing, 60–61; summary of, 62–63; talent, 142–143; targeting of performance related to, 60–61; tools to compensate for lack of, 57–59
tangible rewards, 156, 159–160, 165–166

targeted areas: description of, 20, 25; lack of talent or fit for, 49–50, 60
technical skills, 144
Thematic Apperception Test, 53
time: management of, 23–24, 203; as resource, 90–91, 93
tools and resources: access to people, 91, 93; case study of, 100–101; creative workarounds, 96–98; definition of, 33, 88–92; employee access to, 93–94; employee self-assessments, 99; examples of, 92; exemplary strength and, 94–95; expandable strength and, 92–94, 96; financial resources, 90, 93, 98; information, 91, 93; leveraging of strengths, 97, 203–204; overview of, 87–88; questions for diagnosing, 220; responsibility for addressing, 98–99; summary of, 101; time as resource, 90–91, 93; tools, 89, 95–97; types of, 92
training, 13–14, 149–150, 153
transfer of strengths, 29
trust, 38

V
Vroom, Victor, 158

W
weaknesses, 28, 178, 182
Wonderlic Personnel Test, 52
work environment: interpersonal relationships, 68–69; organizational culture, 66–68; past-and-present-events component of, 71; policies and procedures, 68; workplace design, 69–70
workplace: assessment of, 77; climate in, 70–71; design of, 69–70; policy manual regarding, 78; redesign of, 77
workplace cultural preferences surveys, 51